The Magic Tree

The Magic Tree

poems of fantasy and mystery

chosen by **David Woolger**

Oxford University Press

Oxford University Press, Walton Street, Oxford OX2 6DP

London Glasgow New York Toronto
Delhi Bombay Calcutta Madras Karachi
Nairobi Dar es Salaam Cape Town Salisbury
Kuala Lumpur Singapore Hong Kong Tokyo
Melbourne Auckland

and associate companies in
Beirut Berlin Ibadan Mexico City

British Library Cataloguing in Publication Data

The Magic tree.
 1. Poetry and magic
 I. Woolger, David
 821'.008'037 PN1077
 ISBN 0–19–276046–7

Typeset by Keyspools Ltd,
Bridge Street, Golborne, Lancs
Printed in Great Britain by
Spottiswoode Ballantyne Ltd, Colchester

Contents

The Paint Box

'Cobalt and umber and ultramarine,
Ivory black and emerald green—
What shall I paint to give pleasure to you?'
'Paint for me somebody utterly new.'

'I have painted you tigers in crimson and white.'
'The colours were good and you painted aright.'
'I have painted the cook and a camel in blue
And a panther in purple.' 'You painted them true.

Now mix me a colour that nobody knows,
And paint me a country where nobody goes,
And put in it people a little like you,
Watching a unicorn drinking the dew.'

E. V. Rieu

Visitors

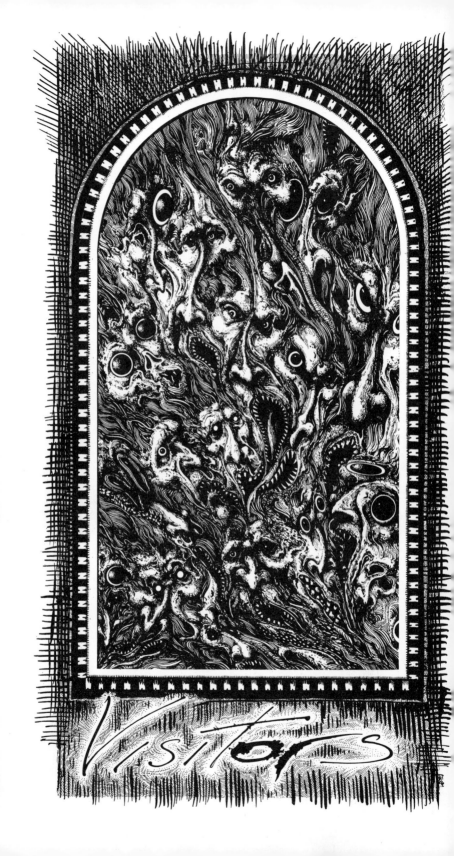

Who's That?

Who's that
stopping at
my door in the
dark, deep
in the dead of the moonless night?

Who's
that in the quiet
blackness,
darker than dark?

Who
turns the han-
dle of my door, who
turns the old brass hand-
le of
my door with never a sound, the handle
that always
creaks and rattles and
squeaks but
now
turns
without a sound, slowly
slowly
   slowly
     round?

Who's that moving through the floor
as if it were a lake, an open door? Who
is it who passes through
what can never be passed through,
who passes through
the rocking-chair
without rocking it,
who passes through
the table without knocking it, who
walks out of the cupboard without unlocking it?
Who's that? Who plays with my toys
with no noise, no
noise?

Who's that? Who is it
silent and silver
as things in mirrors, who's

as slow as feathers,
shy as the shivers,
light as a fly?

Who's that who's that
as close as
close as a hug, a kiss—

Who's THIS?

James Kirkup

The Wind Tapped Like a Tired Man

The Wind—tapped like a tired Man—
And like a Host—'Come in'
I boldly answered—entered then
My Residence within

A Rapid—footless Guest—
To offer whom a Chair
Were as impossible as hand
A Sofa to the Air—

No Bone had He to bind Him—
His Speech was like the Push
Of numerous Humming Birds at once
From a superior Bush—

His Countenance—a Billow—
His Fingers, as He passed
Let go a music—as of tunes
Blown tremulous in Glass—

He visited—still flitting—
Then like a timid Man
Again, He tapped—'twas flurriedly—
And I became alone—

Emily Dickinson

Mary's Ghost

'Twas in the middle of the night,
    To sleep young William tried,
When Mary's ghost came stealing in,
    And stood at his bedside.

O William dear! O William dear!
    My rest eternal ceases;
Alas! my everlasting peace
    Is broken into pieces!

I thought the last of all my cares
    Would end with my last minute;
But, though I went to my long home,
    I didn't stay long in it.

The body-snatchers they have come,
    And made a snatch at me;
It's very hard them kind of men
    Won't let a body be.

You thought that I was buried deep,
    Quite decent like and chary,
But from her grave in Mary-Bone
    They've come and boned your Mary.

The arm that used to take your arm
    Is took to Dr Vyse;
And both my legs are gone to walk
    The hospital at Guy's.

I vowed that you should have my hand,
    But fate gives us denial;
You'll find it there, at Dr Bell's
    In spirits and a phial.

As for my feet, the little feet,
    You used to call so pretty,
There's one, I know, in Bedford Row,
    The t'other's in the City.

I can't tell where my head is gone,
    But Dr Carpune can;
As for my trunk, it's all packed up
    To go by Pickford's van.

I wish you'd go to Mr P
    And save me such a ride;
I don't half like the outside place
    They've took for my inside.

The cock it crows—I must be gone!
    My William, we must part!
But I'll be yours in death, although
    Sir Astley has my heart.

Don't go to weep upon my grave
    And think that there I be:
They haven't left an atom there
    Of my anatomy.

Thomas Hood

Green Man in the Garden

Green man in the garden
    Staring from the tree,
Why do you look so long and hard
    Through the pane at me?

Your eyes are dark as holly,
    Of sycamore your horns,
Your bones are made of elder-branch,
    Your teeth are made of thorns.

Your hat is made of ivy-leaf,
    Of bark your dancing shoes,
And evergreen and green and green
    Your jacket and shirt and trews.

Leave your house and leave your land
    And throw away the key,
And never look behind, he creaked,
    And come and live with me.

I bolted up the window,
    I bolted up the door,
I drew the blind that I should find
    The green man never more.

But when I softly turned the stair
    As I went up to bed,
I saw the green man standing there.
    'Sleep well, my friend,' he said.

Charles Causley

The Visit

The keskidee calls stubbornly
From the lianas. A scramble of brambles
Tries the shut door.

Nobody in.
Perhaps there's been a gold rush,
Or something. This is a dead town.

But there's this clock,
Still ticking. And there's this stable
With the fresh smell of dung. Perhaps they'll be back

Soon.
So the stranger on horseback, in formal black,
Waited with an emissary's

Patience, while
The clock ticked and the stable dried,
The worms gained, and even the door

Fell in suddenly, on a clean, well-lighted
Place—

Then, as great birds came gliding in
Through the stretched jaws
Of the valley,

He was sure, and he turned,
Slapped leather twice
And rode off, his slowly cantering horse

Raising no echoes nor planting the least
Hoofprints in the indifferent clay . . .

Wayne Brown

The Listeners

'Is there anybody there?' said the Traveller,
 Knocking on the moonlit door;
And his horse in the silence champed the grasses
 Of the forest's ferny floor:
And a bird flew out of the turret,
 Above the Traveller's head:
And he smote upon the door again a second time;
 'Is there anybody there?' he said.
But no one descended to the Traveller;
 No head from the leaf-fringed sill
Leaned over and looked into his grey eyes,
 Where he stood perplexed and still.
But only a host of phantom listeners
 That dwelt in the lone house then
Stood listening in the quiet of the moonlight
 To that voice from the world of men:
Stood thronging the faint moonbeams on the dark stair,
 That goes down to the empty hall,
Hearkening in an air stirred and shaken
 By the lonely Traveller's call.
And he felt in his heart their strangeness,
 Their stillness answering his cry,
While his horse moved, cropping the dark turf,
 'Neath the starred and leafy sky;
For he suddenly smote on the door, even
 Louder, and lifted his head:—
'Tell them I came, and no one answered,
 That I kept my word,' he said.
Never the least stir made the listeners,
 Though every word he spake
Fell echoing through the shadowiness of the still house
 From the one man left awake:
Ay, they heard his foot upon the stirrup,
 And the sound of iron on stone,
And how the silence surged softly backward,
 When the plunging hoofs were gone.

Walter de la Mare

Transformations

Transformations

Kemp Owyne

Her mother died when she was young,
    Which gave her cause to make great moan;
Her father married the worst woman
    That ever lived in Christendom.

She served that woman foot and hand,
    In every way she served could be,
Till, once, that woman took her up
    And threw her over Craigy's sea.

Said: 'Lie you there, dove Isabel,
    And all thy sorrows lie with thee;
Till Kemp Owyne come o'er the sea,
    And ransom you with kisses three—
Let all the world do what they will,
    Oh, ransomed shall you never be!'

Her breath grew strong, her hair grew long,
    And twisted thrice about the tree;
And all the people, far and near,
    Thought that a savage beast was she.
This news did come to Kemp Owyne,
    Where he did live, beyond the sea.

He hasted him to Craigy's sea,
    And on the savage beast look'd he;
Her breath was strong, her hair was long,
    And twisted was about the tree,
And with a swing she came about:
    'Come to Craigy's sea, and kiss with me!'

'Here is a royal belt,' she cried,
    'That I have found in the deep green sea,
And while your body it is on,
    Drawn shall your blood never be;
But if you touch me, tail or fin,
    I vow my belt your death shall be.'

He stepped right in, gave her a kiss,
    The royal belt away took he;
Her breath was strong, her hair was long,
    And twisted twice about the tree,
And with a swing she came about:
    'Come to Craigy's sea, and kiss with me!'

'Here is a royal ring,' she said,
    'That I have found in the deep green sea,
And while your finger it is on,
    Drawn shall your blood never be;
But if you touch me, tail or fin,
    I swear my ring your death shall be.'

He stepped right in, gave her a kiss,
    The royal ring away took he;
Her breath was strong, her hair was long,
    And twisted once about the tree,
And with a swing she came about:
    'Come to Craigy's sea, and kiss with me!'

'Here is a royal sword,' she said,
    'That I have found in the deep green sea,
And while your body it is on,
    Drawn shall your blood never be;
But if you touch me, tail or fin,
    I swear my sword your death shall be.'

He stepped right in, gave her a kiss,
    The royal sword away took he;
Her breath was sweet, her hair grew short,
    And twisted none about the tree,
And smilingly she came about,
    As fair a woman as fair could be.

Anon

Hasana's Lover

You girls who cast your eyes about
    To catch a handsome man,
Come, hear the tale of Hasana
    And how her love began.

She stepped into the market place
    And held her head up high:
While others smiled with downcast eyes,
    She stared about the sky.

She levelled her eyes about the place
    But sought no husband there:
'Rather than marry one of you
    I'd shave off half my hair.'

'I'd rather live in prison bonds
    Or rot inside my grave,
Than marry a single one of you,
    And live and die a slave.'

Her father whipped her on the back,
    Her mother groaned aloud,
Yet never a man Hasana took,
    Hasana was so proud.

But pride's a sin, old time will win,
    And walking through the town,
Hasana saw a man so fine
    He might have worn a crown.

He might have sat upon a throne
    And ruled the lives of men,
And he cast his eyes on Hasana,
    And she never looked up again.

She turned her eyes down to the ground
    And followed a pace behind,
And wherever he went she followed him
    As if her eyes were blind.

She moved with him as a shadow moves,
    As a shadow pale and dim,
And if ever she raised her downcast eyes
    They rose to look at him.

They asked the stranger for his name,
  But never a name gave he:
And all the words he ever spoke—
  'She's a fool that follows me.'

The stranger strode from out the town
  Hasana followed still,
Her father roared, her mother wept,
  Hasana had her will.

The stranger strode on the narrow paths,
  His stride was strong and free,
And all the words he ever spoke—
  'She's a fool that follows me.'

They came upon a legless man
  Who sat beside the way,
And he stopped before that legless man—
  'There's a debt that I must pay.'

He tore the legs from off his trunk
  To give to the legless man:
'Thanks for the loan of these your limbs,'
  The stranger then began—

'A girl must pay to have her way
  And follow a man like me.'
Then he turned and smiled at his own dear love,
  And she wished that she were free.

She looked with fear at her husband dear,
  But she could not run for fright,
So she followed the man with the crippled stumps
  As he stumbled through the night.

They came upon an armless man
  Who sat beside the way,
And he stopped before that armless man—
  'There's a debt that I must pay.'

He tore the arms from off his trunk
  To give to the armless man:
'Thanks for the loan of these your limbs,'
  The stranger then began—

'A girl who loves a legless man
  Won't miss a pair of arms.'

And he turned and smiled at his own dear love,
    Displaying all his charms.

She looked with fear at her husband dear,
    But she could not run for fright:
For better to go with one you know
    Than back into that night.

So he gave back the body of man
    That never had been his own:
He gave the heart out of his breast,
    He gave the tall back bone.

'A girl who follows a handsome face
    Is as wise as any child.'
So the head rolled on before the girl,
    And caught her eyes and smiled.

'Soon we'll be home my dearest love,
    And you shall share my bed.'
But proud Hasana moaned and wept
    And wished that she were dead.

They came to a man who had no face,
    Sat there beside the way:
And he stopped before that faceless man,
    And he gave his flesh away.

So now she knew her lover's name,
    No need had she to ask!
On his narrow bed in the bitter earth
    She performed her wifely task.

She lay in fear by that husband dear,
    For the bone has a cold embrace,
When life is done and beauty's gone
    In a cold and lonely place.

I swear to you my tale is true,
    And was since time began;
If you can't tell what's in my mind,
    Perhaps your mothers can.

For love is like a pleasant flower
    To pluck before it's grown,
But there are thorns in that bonny bush
    Will prick you to the bone.

Paul Edwards

The Wizard

The wizard, watchful, waits alone
within his tower of cold gray stone
and ponders in his wicked way
what evil deeds he'll do this day.
He's tall and thin, with wrinkled skin,
a tangled beard hangs from his chin,
his cheeks are gaunt, his eyes set deep,
he scarcely eats, he needs no sleep.
> His fingers wave arcane commands,
> ten bony sticks on withered hands,
> his flowing cloak is smirched with grime,
> he's worn it since the dawn of time.
> Upon his hat, in silver lines
> are pictured necromantic signs,
> symbols of the awesome power
> of the wizard, alone in his cold stone tower.
He scans his mystic stock in trade—
charms to fetch a demon's aid,
seething stews of purplish potions,
throbbing thaumaturgic lotions,
supernatural tracts and tomes
replete with lore of elves and gnomes,
talismans, amulets, willowy wand
to summon spirits from beyond.

He spies a bullfrog by the door
and stooping, scoops it off the floor.
He flicks his wand, the frog's a flea
through elemental sorcery,
the flea hops once, the flea hops twice,
the flea becomes a pair of mice
that dive into a bubbling brew,
emerging as one cockatoo.
> The wizard laughs a hollow laugh,
> the soaking bird's reduced by half,
> and when, perplexed, it starts to squawk,
> the wizard turns it into chalk
> with which he deftly writes a spell
> that makes the chalk a silver bell
> which tinkles in the ashen air
> till flash . . . a fire burns brightly there.
He gestures with an ancient knack
to try to bring the bullfrog back.

Another flash! ... no flame now burns
as once again the frog returns,
but when it bounds about in fear,
the wizard shouts, 'Begone from here,'
and midway through a frightened croak
it vanishes in clouds of smoke.
　　The wizard smirks a fiendish smirk
　　reflecting on the woes he'll work
　　as he consults a dusty text
　　and checks which hex he'll conjure next.
　　He may pluck someone off the spot
　　and turn him into ... who knows what?
　　Should you encounter a toad or lizard,
　　look closely ... it may be the work of the wizard.

Jack Prelutsky

The Two Witches

O, sixteen hundred and ninety one,
Never was year so well begun,
Backsy-forsy and inside-out,
The best of all years to ballad about.

On the first fine day of January
I ran to my sweetheart Margery
And tossed her over the roof so far
That down she fell like a shooting star.

But when we two had frolicked and kissed
She clapped her fingers about my wrist
And tossed me over the chimney stack,
And danced on me till my bones did crack.

Then, when she had laboured to ease my pain,
We sat by the stile of Robin's Lane,
She in a hare and I in a toad
And puffed at the clouds till merry they glowed.

We spelled our loves until close of day.
I wished her good-night and walked away,
But she put out a tongue that was long and red
And swallowed me down like a crumb of bread.

Robert Graves　　　　　　　　　　　　　　　　　29

Allison Gross

O Allison Gross, that lives in yon tower,
    The ugliest witch in the north country,
She enticed me one day up to her bower,
    And many fair speeches she made to me.

She stroked my head, and she combed my hair,
    And she set me down softly on her knee;
Said: 'If you will be my love so true,
    Many fine things I will give to thee.'

She showed me a mantle of red scarlet,
    With golden flowers and fringes fine;
Said: 'If you will be my love so true,
    This goodly gift it shall be thine.'

'Away, away, you ugly witch,
    Hold far away, and let me be!
I never will be your love so true,
    And I wish I were out of your company.'

She next brought a shirt of the softest silk,
    Well wrought with pearls about the band;
Said: 'If you will be my love so true,
    This goodly gift you shall command.'

She showed me a cup of the good red gold,
    Well set with jewels so fair to see;
Said: 'If you will be my love so true,
    This goodly gift I will give to thee.'

'Away, away, you ugly witch,
    Hold far away, and let me be!
For I would not kiss your ugly mouth
    For all the gifts you give to me.'

She turned her right and round about,
    And thrice she blew on a grass-green horn,
And she swore by the moon and stars above
    That she'd make me rue the day I was born.

Then out did she take a silver wand,
    And she turned her three times round and round;
She muttered such words that my strength did fail,
    And I fell down senseless to the ground.

She turned me into an ugly worm,
    And made me toddle about the tree;
And aye, on every Saturday's night,
    My sister Maisry came to me,

With silver basin and silver comb,
    To comb my head upon her knee;
But before I had kissed her ugly mouth,
    I'd rather have toddled about the tree.

But as it fell out, on last Hallow-e'en,
    When the fairy court was riding by,
The queen lighted down on a flowery bank
    Not far from the tree where I used to lie.

She took me up in her milk-white hand,
    And she stroked me three times on her knee;
She changed me again to my own proper shape,
    And I no more must toddle about the tree.

Anon

An Old Man sat in a Waterfall

An old man sat in a waterfall
    And the water dripped through his hair;
His voice was green as a sea-pie's call:
'Come weeds, and turf my skull,
For my hair is loosed by the bite of the beck—
    Soon my head will be bare;
    I'll have no pride at all.

'Come wagtail, water-ousel sing
    And bubble in my throat;
Come water-rat skulk in my breast,
My flesh shall be your winter coat;
Come water-hen and make your nest
    In hollows of my ribs;
There you'll find a place to play,
For life has rotted my heart away.'

The old man sat in the waterfall
And the water turned his skin to bone.
Stalactites hung from his chin like a beard;
    His shoulders were shelled with stone.
And leaves in autumn drop from tall
Arthritic thorn-trees by the limestone wall
On the old stone man in the waterfall.

Norman Nicholson

Ghosts

GHOSTS

Emperors of the Island

There is the story of a deserted island
where five men walked down to the bay.

The story of this island is
that three men would two men slay.

Three men dug two graves in the sand,
three men stood on the sea wet rock,
three shadows moved away.

There is the story of a deserted island
where three men walked down to the bay.

The story of this island is
that two men would one man slay.

Two men dug one grave in the sand,
two men stood on the sea wet rock,
two shadows moved away.

There is the story of a deserted island
where two men walked down to the bay.

The story of this island is
that one man would one man slay.

One man dug one grave in the sand,
one man stood on the sea wet rock,
one shadow moved away.

There is the story of a deserted island
where four ghosts walked down to the bay.

The story of this island is
that four ghosts would one man slay.

Four ghosts dug one grave in the sand,
four ghosts stood on the sea wet rock;
five ghosts moved away.

Dannie Abse

Old Roger is Dead and Laid in his Grave

Old Roger is dead and laid in his grave,
   Laid in his grave, laid in his grave;
Old Roger is dead and laid in his grave,
   H'm ha! laid in his grave.

They planted an apple tree over his head,
   Over his head, over his head;
They planted an apple tree over his head,
   H'm ha! over his head.

The apples grew ripe and ready to fall,
   Ready to fall, ready to fall;
The apples grew ripe and ready to fall,
   H'm ha! ready to fall.

There came an old woman a-picking them all,
   A-picking them all, a-picking them all;
There came an old woman a-picking them all,
   H'm ha! picking them all.

Old Roger jumps up and gives her a knock,
   Gives her a knock, gives her a knock;
Which makes the old woman go hipperty-hop,
   H'm ha! hipperty-hop.

Anon

When the Night Wind Howls

When the night wind howls in the chimney cowls,
    and the bat in the moonlight flies,
And inky clouds, like funeral shrouds,
    sail over the midnight skies—
When the footpads quail at the night-bird's wail,
    and black dogs bay at the moon,
Then is the spectres' holiday—
    then is the ghosts' high-noon!

Ha! Ha!
Then is the ghosts' high-noon!

As the sob of the breeze sweeps over the trees,
    and the mists lie low on the fen,
From grey tomb-stones are gathered the bones
    that once were women and men,
And away they go, with a mop and a mow,
    to the revel that ends too soon,
For cockcrow limits our holiday—
    the dead of the night's high-noon!

Ha! Ha!
The dead of the night's high-noon!

And then each ghost with his ladye-toast
    to their churchyard beds takes flight,
With a kiss, perhaps, on her lantern chaps,
    and a grisly grim 'good-night'!
Till the welcome knell of the midnight bell
    rings forth its jolliest tune,
And ushers in our next high holiday—
    the dead of the night's high-noon!

Ha! Ha!
The dead of the night's high-noon!

W. S. Gilbert

Colonel Fazackerley

Colonel Fazackerley Butterworth-Toast
Bought an old castle complete with a ghost,
But someone or other forgot to declare
To Colonel Fazack that the spectre was there.

On the very first evening, while waiting to dine,
The Colonel was taking a fine sherry wine,
When the ghost, with a furious flash and a flare,
Shot out of the chimney and shivered, 'Beware!'

Colonel Fazackerley put down his glass
And said, 'My dear fellow, that's really first class!
I just can't conceive how you do it at all.
I imagine you're going to a Fancy Dress Ball?'

At this, the dread ghost gave a withering cry.
Said the Colonel (his monocle firm in his eye),
'Now just how you do it I wish I could think.
Do sit down and tell me, and please have a drink.'

The ghost in his phosphorous cloak gave a roar
And floated about between ceiling and floor.
He walked through a wall and returned through a pane
And backed up the chimney and came down again.

Said the Colonel, 'With laughter I'm feeling quite weak!'
(As trickles of merriment ran down his cheek).
'My house-warming party I hope you won't spurn.
You *must* say you'll come and you'll give us a turn!'

At this, the poor spectre—quite out of his wits—
Proceeded to shake himself almost to bits.
He rattled his chains and he clattered his bones
And he filled the whole castle with mumbles and moans.

But Colonel Fazackerley, just as before,
Was simply delighted and called out, 'Encore!'
At which the ghost vanished, his efforts in vain,
And never was seen at the castle again.

'Oh dear, what a pity!' said Colonel Fazack.
'I don't know his name, so I can't call him back.'
And then with a smile that was hard to define,
Colonel Fazackerley went in to dine.

Charles Causley

The Old Wife and the Ghost

There was an old wife and she lived all alone
    In a cottage not far from Hitchin:
And one bright night, by the full moon light,
    Comes a ghost right into her kitchen.

About that kitchen neat and clean
    The ghost goes pottering round.
But the poor old woman is deaf as a boot
    And so hears never a sound.

The ghost blows up the kitchen fire,
    As bold as bold can be;
He helps himself from the larder shelf,
    But never a sound hears she.

He blows on his hands to make them warm,
    And whistles aloud 'Whee-hee!'
But still as a sack the old soul lies
    And never a sound hears she.

From corner to corner he runs about,
    And into the cupboard he peeps;
He rattles the door and bumps on the floor,
    But still the old wife sleeps.

Jangle and bang go the pots and pans,
    As he throws them all around;
And the plates and mugs and dishes and jugs,
    He flings them all to the ground.

Madly the ghost tears up and down
    And screams like a storm at sea;
And at last the old wife stirs in her bed—
    And it's 'Drat those mice,' says she.

Then the first cock crows and morning shows
    And the troublesome ghost's away.
But oh! what a pickle the poor wife sees
    When she gets up next day.

'Them's tidy big mice,' the old wife thinks,
    And off she goes to Hitchin,
And a tidy big cat she fetches back
    To keep the mice from her kitchen.

James Reeves

Tom

The farmhand Tom, with his apple and turnip face,
Grumbles, grins and groans through the long summer hours,
Reviles St Martin, by whose grace
Thus he must plod through the poppies and cornflowers.
Night is a stretch of dead and drear slumber,
Then up again, and again he must lumber
Into his clothes and away through the park,
Carrying pails,
              Must wade through the dark.
Till even the comforting darkness fails,
Tousled and blinking,
Clanking and clinking,
A very robust
Traditional ghost:
    For clanking and lank
    The Armoured Knight
    Rides down the dank
    Shadows in flight;
    Grass stiff with frost
    Shows grey as steel
    As the Conquering Ghost
    Clanks down the hill.
        Now the first cock crows,
        Impudent, frightened, through the dark;
        Then a cold wind blows,
    And that whining dog, Dawn, begins to bark.
Then the Knight in Armour
Passes away,
As the growing clamour
Proclaims, 'It is Day.'
The trees grow taller,
The gate is shut.
The Knight grows smaller,
              Goes smaller,
                  And out.

Osbert Sitwell

Dicky

Mother: Oh, what a heavy sigh!
      Dicky, are you ailing?

Dicky: Even by the fireside, Mother,
      My heart is failing.

Tonight across the down,
    Whistling and jolly,
I sauntered out from town
    With my stick of holly.

Bounteous and cool from sea
    The wind was blowing,
Cloud shadows under the moon
    Coming and going.

I sang old country songs,
    Ran and leaped quick,
And turned home by St Swithin's
    Twirling my stick.

And there, as I was passing
    The churchyard gate,
An old man stopped me: 'Dicky,
    You're walking late.'

I did not know the man,
    I grew afeared
At his lean, lolling jaw,
    His spreading beard.

His garments old and musty,
    Of antique cut,
His body very frail and bony,
    His eyes tight shut.

Oh, even to tell it now
    My courage ebbs . . .
His face was clay, Mother,
    His beard, cobwebs.

In that long horrid pause
    'Good night,' he said,
Entered and clicked the gate:
    'Each to his bed.'

Mother: Do not sigh or fear, Dicky;
          How is it right
       To grudge the dead their ghostly dark
          And wan moonlight?

       We have the glorious sun,
          Lamp and fireside.
       Grudge not the dead their moonbeams
          When abroad they ride.

       Robert Graves

Song of the Fishing Ghosts

Night is the time when phantoms play,
   Flows the river,
   Phantoms white
   Phantoms black
Fish in the dark salt water bay.

Skulls are nets for phantom fishers,
   Flows the river,
Phantoms red on a phantom river
   Dark flows the river.

Black phantom splashes
   Flows the river
White phantom splashes
   Flows the river.

Night is the time when phantoms play,
   Heads are nets
   For phantom fishers
There on the dark salt water bay.

   Phantoms black
   Phantoms red
   Phantoms white
   For nets their heads
And the dark, dark, dark river flows.

Efua Sutherland

No Room for Ghosts

This house has no room for ghosts.
Neither periwigged gentlemen,
Spectres, nor skeletons
Clanging their scrap-iron
May tramp through the hall.
This house has no corners
For hiding the dead,
No cupboards or passages, cellars or holes in the wall,
For the shadowy gentlemen
To step into, removing their head
As the landlady passes.
And the pale half-witted
Possible murdered or even
Never existent uncle of whom we hear
Isn't welcome or even permitted
To re-appear.

This house is too full of noises,
Of children and cooking, armchairs, insistences, ructions,
Baked apples and broken appointments. There isn't a corner,
A moment, a shelf in the cupboard,
Or even a space in the cellar,
For phantoms and recollections.
There are too many words
For the past to be heard.
No one attends to the caller.

So mediums, goblins and revenants,
However well recommended
By curiosity, fate,
Guilt, or the S.P.R.,
No rapping on tables here:
No one's sufficiently bored.
Poltergeists, do not throw plates
To prove that you love us; and bogies,
Incubi, succubi, memories,
Get this in your empty heads—
You'll be ignored, ignored.
Leave us alone in our beds.
Go elsewhere, do not call here.

Laurence Lerner

Two's Company

The sad story of the man who didn't believe in ghosts

They said the house was haunted, but
He laughed at them and said, 'Tut, tut!
I've never heard such tittle-tattle
As ghosts that groan and chains that rattle;
And just to prove I'm in the right,
Please leave me here to spend the night.'

They winked absurdly, tried to smother
Their ignorant laughter, nudged each other,
And left him just as dusk was falling
With a hunchback moon and screech-owls calling.
Not that this troubled him one bit;
In fact, he was quite glad of it,
Knowing it's every sane man's mission
To contradict all superstition.

But what is that? Outside it seemed
As if chains rattled, someone screamed!
Come, come, it's merely nerves, he's certain
(But just the same, he draws the curtain).
The stroke of twelve—but there's no clock!
He shuts the door and turns the lock
(Of course, he knows that no one's there,
But no harm's done by taking care!)
Someone's outside—the silly joker,
(He may as well pick up the poker!)
That noise again! He checks the doors,
Shutters the windows, makes a pause
To seek the safest place to hide—
(The cupboard's strong—he creeps inside).
'Not that there's anything to fear,'
He tells himself, when at his ear
A voice breathes softly, 'How do you do!
I am the ghost. Pray, who are you?'

Raymond Wilson

Royal Persons

Royal Persons

The Three Singing Birds

The King walked in his garden green,
 Where grew a marvellous tree;
And out of its leaves came singing birds
 By one, and two, and three.

The first bird had wings of white,
 The second had wings of gold,
The third had wings of deepest blue
 Most beauteous to behold.

The white bird flew to the northern land,
 The gold bird flew to the west,
The blue bird flew to the cold, cold south
 Where never bird might nest.

The King waited a twelvemonth long,
 Till back the three birds flew,
They lighted down upon the tree,
 The white, the gold, and the blue.

The white bird brought a pearly seed
 And gave it to the King;
The gold bird from out of the west
 He brought a golden ring.

The third bird with feathers blue
 Who came from the far cold south,
A twisted sea-shell smooth and grey
 He carried in his mouth.

The King planted the pearly seed
 Down in his garden green,
And up there sprang a pearl-white maid,
 The fairest ever seen.

She looked at the King and knelt her down
 All under the magic tree,
She smiled at him with her red lips
 But not a word said she.

Instead she took the grey sea-shell
 And held it to his ear,
She pressed it close and soon the King
 A strange, sweet song did hear.

He raised the fair maid by the hand
    Until she stood at his side;
Then he gave her the golden ring
    And took her for his bride.

And at their window sang the birds,
    They sang the whole night through,
Then off they went at break of day,
    The white, the gold, and the blue.

James Reeves

A Spell for Sleeping

Sweet william, silverweed, sally-my-handsome.
Dimity darkens the pittering water.
On gloomed lawns wanders a king's daughter.

Curtains are clouding the casement windows.
A moon-glade smurrs the lake with light.
Doves cover the tower with quiet.

Three owls whit-whit in the withies.
Seven fish in a deep pool shimmer.
The princess moves to the spiral stair.

Slowly the sickle moon mounts up.
Frogs hump under moss and mushroom.
The princess climbs to her high hushed room,

Step by step to her shadowed tower.
Water laps the white lake shore.
A ghost opens the princess's door.

    Seven fish in the sway of the water.
    Six candles for a king's daughter.
    Five sighs for a drooping head.
    Four ghosts to gentle her bed.
    Three owls in the dusk falling.
    Two tales to be telling.
    One spell for sleeping.

Tamarisk, trefoil, tormentil.
Sleep rolls down from the clouded hill.
A princess dreams of a silver pool.

The moonlight spreads, the soft ferns flitter.
Stilled in a shimmering drift of water,
Seven fish dream of a lost king's daughter.

Alastair Reid

The King of China's Daughter

The King of China's daughter,
She never would love me
Though I hung my cap and bells upon
Her nutmeg tree.
For oranges and lemons,
The stars in bright blue air
(I stole them long ago my dear),
Were dangling there.
The Moon did give me silver pence,
The Sun did give me gold,
And both together softly blew
And made my porridge cold;
But the King of China's daughter
Pretended not to see
Where I hung my cap and bells upon
Her nutmeg tree.

The King of China's daughter,
So beautiful to see
With her face like yellow water, left
Her nutmeg tree.
Her little rope for skipping
She kissed and gave it me—
Made of painted notes of singing-birds
Among the fields of tea.
I skipped across the nutmeg grove,
I skipped across the sea;
But neither sun nor moon, my dear,
Has yet caught me.

Edith Sitwell

The Ice King

Where the world is grey and lone
Sits the Ice King on his throne—

Passionless, austere, afar,
Underneath the Polar Star.

Over all his splendid plains
An eternal stillness reigns.

Silent creatures of the North,
White and strange and fierce, steal forth:

Soft-foot beasts from frozen lair,
Noiseless birds that wing the air,

Souls of seamen dead, who lie
Stark beneath the pale north sky;

Shapes to living eye unknown,
Wild and shy, come round the throne

Where the Ice King sits in view
To receive their homage due.

But the Ice King's quiet eyes,
Calm, implacable, and wise,

Gaze beyond the silent throng,
With a steadfast look and long,

Down to where the summer streams
Murmur in their golden dreams;

Where the sky is rich and deep,
Where warm stars bring down warm sleep,

Where the days are, every one,
Clad with warmth and crowned with sun.

And the longing gods may feel
Stirs within his heart of steel,

And he yearns far forth to go
From his land of ice and snow.

But forever, grey and lone,
Sits the Ice King on his throne—

Passionless, austere, afar,
Underneath the Polar Star.

A. B. Demille   51

The Fish King's Stolen Daughter

I am King in the Land of Forsaken Fishnets
five fathoms under the green skin of the sea
mermaids ply me with oysters in amethyst pudding bowls
lost figureheads comb my hair
nymphs sit on my knee

I once had a Princess who was my beloved dark daughter
she was dragged from the shore by the White Wolf Wind
when last I saw her she was drifting upwards through the water
her shell-bag by her side
waving her hand

Now I study each night my dolphin zodiac
or call from his far-off cell Mandragora my sorcerer
he holds a bubble close to his squinting eyes
and in a dim voice says:
'I see her sitting in shadows beneath ancient trees'

'Will she return, ah, will she return?' I cry
'She will return when orchards grow under the sea
Until that time you will dream alone'
The mermaids float round me with worried frowns
they offer me shrimp-cakes and sapphires and lovingbones
but I shake my head, strumming idly a forlorn tune
as I sniff the air for the scent of apple bloom

Cara Lockhart Smith

Once I was a Monarch's Daughter

Once I was a monarch's daughter,
    And sat on a lady's knee;
But am now a nightly rover,
    Banished to the ivy tree.
Crying hoo, hoo, hoo, hoo, hoo, hoo,
    Hoo, hoo, hoo, my feet are cold.
Pity me, for here you see me
    Persecuted, poor, and old.

Anon

King Whirligig

This is the prancing snacker-King
Whose sideways eyes are blazy-O
And when the ducklings see him pass
They scuttle off like crazy-O
    'Oh luffly ducks, oh fluffly ducks
    Why would I harm thy flocky forms?
    Curr-oop curr-oop my eiderdowns
    Come to the snicker-snacker's arms'
        With a waddle and a flap in the mist so far
        The King is not where the ducklings are

This is the slinking snacker-King
Whose sideways eyes are killy-O
And when the ravens see him pass
They clatter off like billy-O

    'Oh ravens meaty, ravens sleek
    Why would I harm thy ruffian forms
    Kar-kark kar-kark my feather hat
    Come to the snicker-snacker's arms'
        With a croak and a krawk in the mist so far
        The King is not where the ravens are

The castle stark in the green-dark air
Is lit by a first faint frosty star
The windless night is cold and bare
But the King is not where the birdies are

Cara Lockhart Smith

Queen Whirligig

The Queen is a lardy dardy lady
Indeed she is and cuckoo too
Mind as closed as a lidless casket
Heart as tight as a screw
   Singing drearly the old flam flim
   She stalks the corridors white and dim
     'Tis the mewing bats in the belfry she hears
     And the howl of the Dorking fowl

The Queen was never as fresh as a flower
She'll never wear down like stone
She'll be the same through the musty hours
As a bone to another bone
   Singing drearly the Moon Wood hymn
   She stalks the corridors white and dim
     'Tis the bark of the dog in the ebony park
     She hears, and the howl of the fowl

    Oval owled
    Dungeon cold
    Batty old
    Tom Bedlam mould

   Topsy-turvy she turns the chair
   With her long and wrinkeldy hands
   Bustling big as a laundry bag
   With her hair in rubber bands

Cara Lockhart Smith

Fairies and other Sprites

Fairies and
other Spri

The Fairies

Up the airy mountain,
    Down the rushy glen,
We daren't go a-hunting
    For fear of little men;
Wee folk, good folk,
    Trooping all together;
Green jacket, red cap,
    And white owl's feather!

Down along the rocky shore
    Some make their home,
They live on crispy pancakes
    Of yellow tide-foam;
Some in the reeds
    Of the black mountain-lake,
With frogs for their watchdogs,
    All night awake.

High on the hill-top
    The old King sits;
He is now so old and grey
    He's nigh lost his wits.
With a bridge of white mist
    Columbkill he crosses,
On his stately journeys
    From Slieveleague to Rosses;
Or going up with music
    On cold starry nights,
To sup with the Queen
    Of the gay Northern Lights.

They stole little Bridget
    For seven years long;
When she came down again,
    Her friends were all gone.
They took her lightly back,
    Between the night and morrow,
They thought that she was fast asleep,
    But she was dead with sorrow.
They have kept her ever since
    Deep within the lake,
On a bed of flag-leaves,
    Watching till she wake.

By the craggy hillside,
    Through the mosses bare,
They have planted thorn trees
    For pleasure, here and there.
Is any man so daring
    As dig them up in spite,
He shall find the thornies set
    In his bed at night.

Up the airy mountain,
    Down the rushy glen,
We daren't go a-hunting
    For fear of little men;
Wee folk, good folk,
    Trooping all together;
Green jacket, red cap,
    And white owl's feather!

William Allingham

Puck's Song

Now the hungry lion roars,
    And the wolf behowls the moon;
Whilst the heavy ploughman snores,
    All with weary task fordone.
Now the wasted brands do glow,
    Whilst the screech-owl, screeching loud,
Puts the wretch that lies in woe
    In remembrance of a shroud.
Now it is the time of night
    That the graves, all gaping wide,
Every one lets forth his sprite,
    In the church-way paths to glide:
And we fairies, that do run
    By the triple Hecate's team,
From the presence of the sun,
    Following darkness like a dream,
Now are frolic: not a mouse
Shall disturb this hallow'd house:
I am sent with broom before,
To sweep the dust behind the door.

William Shakespeare

The Fairy Queen

Come, follow, follow me,
    You, fairy elves that be:
    Which circle on the green,
    Come follow Mab your queen.
Hand in hand let's dance around,
For this place is fairy ground.

    When mortals are at rest,
    And snoring in their nest;
    Unheard, and un-espied,
    Through key-holes we do glide;
Over tables, stools and shelves.
We trip it with our fairy elves.

    And, if the house be foul
    With platter, dish or bowl,
    Up stairs we nimbly creep,
    And find the sluts asleep:
There we pinch their arms and thighs;
None escapes, nor none espies.

    But if the house be swept,
    And from uncleanness kept,
    We praise the household maid,
    And duly she is paid:
For we use before we go
To drop a tester in her shoe.

    Upon a mushroom's head
    Our table-cloth we spread;
    A grain of rye, or wheat,
    Is manchet, which we eat;
Pearly drops of dew we drink
In acorn cups fill'd to the brink.

    The brains of nightingales,
    With unctuous fat of snails,
    Between two cockles stew'd,
    Is meat that's easily chew'd;
Tails of worms, and marrow of mice
Do make a dish, that's wondrous nice.

The grasshopper, gnat, and fly,
Serve for our minstrelsy;
Grace said, we dance a while,
And so the time beguile;
And if the moon doth hide her head,
The gloe-worm lights us home to bed.

On tops of dewy grass
So nimbly do we pass,
The young and tender stalk
Ne'er bends when we do walk:
Yet in the morning may be seen
Where we the night before have been.

Anon

Fantasy

I think if I should wait some night in an enchanted forest
With tall dim hemlocks and moss-covered branches,
And quiet, shadowy aisles between the tall blue-lichened trees;
With low shrubs forming grotesque outlines in the moonlight,
And the ground covered with a thick carpet of pine needles
So that my footsteps made no sound,—

They would not be afraid to glide silently from their hiding
        places
To the white patch of moonlight on the pine needles,
And dance to the moon and the stars and the wind.

Their arms would gleam white in the moonlight
And a thousand dewdrops sparkle in the dimness of their hair;
But I should not dare to look at their wildly beautiful faces.

Ruth Mather Skidmore

La Belle Dame sans Merci

O, what can ail thee, knight-at-arms,
  Alone and palely loitering?
The sedge has wither'd from the lake,
  And no birds sing.

O, what can ail thee, knight-at-arms,
  So haggard and so woe-begone?
The squirrel's granary is full,
  And the harvest's done.

I see a lily on thy brow,
  With anguish moist and fever dew;
And on thy cheeks a fading rose
  Fast withereth too.

I met a lady in the meads,
  Full beautiful—a fairy's child;
Her hair was long, her foot was light,
  And her eyes were wild.

I made a garland for her head,
  And bracelets too, and fragrant zone;
She look'd at me as she did love,
  And made sweet moan.

I set her on my pacing steed,
  And nothing else saw all day long;
For sidelong would she bend, and sing
  A fairy's song.

She found me roots of relish sweet,
  And honey wild, and manna dew,
And sure in language strange she said—
  I love thee true.

She took me to her elfin grot,
  And there she wept, and sigh'd full sore,
And there I shut her wild sad eyes
  With kisses four.

And there she lulled me asleep,
  And there I dream'd—Ah! woe betide!
The latest dream I ever dream'd
  On the cold hill side.

I saw pale kings and princes too,
    Pale warriors, death-pale were they all;
They cried—'La Belle Dame sans Merci
    Hath thee in thrall!'

I saw their starved lips in the gloam,
    With horrid warning gaped wide,
And I awoke and found me here,
    On the cold hill's side.

And this is why I sojourn here,
    Alone and palely loitering,
Though the sedge has wither'd from the lake,
    And no birds sing.

John Keats

Water Sprite

You just have to
    start blowing bubbles underwater from the crack of
        dawn,
    stir up ripples all the morning,
    at noontime run the water off your coat-tails on the
        strips between the fields,
        all afternoon tread the mud in wavy ridges,
        at dusk start croaking at the moon,—

    no one has the time today
    just to sit and do a little haunting.

Miroslav Holub

The Crackling Twig

There came a satyr creeping through the wood,
His hair fell on his breast, his legs were slim:
His eyes were dancing wickedly, he stood,
He peeped about on every side of him.

He danced! He peeped! But, at a sound I made,
A crackling twig, he turned; and, suddenly,
In three great jumps, he bounded to the shade,
And disappeared among the greenery!

James Stephens

Overheard on a Saltmarsh

Nymph, nymph, what are your beads?

Green glass, goblin. Why do you stare at them?

Give them me.

    No.

Give them me. Give them me.

      No.

Then I will howl all night in the reeds,
Lie in the mud and howl for them.

Goblin, why do you love them so?

They are better than stars or water,
Better than voices of winds that sing,
Better than any man's fair daughter,
Your green glass beads on a silver ring.

Hush, I stole them out of the moon.

Give me your beads, I desire them.

      No.

I will howl in a deep lagoon
For your green glass beads, I love them so.
Give them me. Give them.

      No.

Harold Monro

How to Treat Elves

I met an elf-man in the woods,
    The wee-est little elf!
Sitting under a mushroom tall—
    'Twas taller than himself!

'How do you do, little elf,' I said,
    'And what do you do all day?'
'I dance 'n fwolic about,' said he,
    ''N scuttle about and play;

'I s'prise the butterflies, 'n when
    A katydid I see,
"Katy didn't!" I say, and he
    Says "Katy did!" to me!

'I hide behind my mushroom stalk
    When Mister Mole comes froo,
'N only jus' to fwighten him
    I jump out 'n say "Boo!"

''N then I swing on a cobweb swing
    Up in the air so high,
'N the cwickets chirp to hear me sing
    "Upsy-daisy-die!"

''N then I play with the baby chicks,
    I call them, chick chick chick!
'N what do you think of that?' said he.
    I said, 'It makes me sick.

'It gives me sharp and shooting pains
    To listen to such drool.'
I lifted up my foot, and squashed
    The God damned little fool.

Morris Bishop

Creatures

CREATURES

The Bogus-boo

The Bogus-boo
Is a creature who
Comes out at night—and why?
He likes the air;
He likes to scare
The nervous passer-by.

Out from the park
At dead of dark
He comes with huffling pad.
If, when alone,
You hear his moan,
'Tis like to drive you mad.

He has two wings,
Pathetic things,
With which he cannot fly.
His tusks look fierce,
Yet could not pierce
The merest butterfly.

He has six ears,
But what he hears
Is very faint and small;
And with the claws
On his eight paws
He cannot scratch at all.

He looks so wise
With his owl-eyes,
His aspect grim and ghoulish;
But truth to tell,
He sees not well
And is distinctly foolish.

This Bogus-boo,
What can he do
But huffle in the dark?
So don't take fright;
He has no bite
And very little bark.

James Reeves

The Horny-goloch

The horny-goloch is an awesome beast,
Soople and scaly;
It has twa horns, an a hantle o feet,
An a forkie tailie.

Anon

How and When and Where and Why

How and when and where and why
stars and sun and moon and sky

canals and craters, dunghills, dunes
tell me what's beyond the moons?

beyond the moons the sands are deep
they spread through all the purple skies
in them are Giants who never sleep
but watch the world with burning eyes

they're just like us, with sharper claws
huger pincers, fiercer jaws
and if they catch you—goodbye head!
goodbye little crystal bed!

so wrap your feelers round your feet
fold your thorax nice and neat
the sun is high, the hour is late
now it's time to estivate

> I lay me in my quartzy pool
> I pray the gods to keep it cool
> to keep off demons far and near
> and wake me when the winter's here
> to dance with joy on all my legs
> and live to lay a thousand eggs

Phyllis Gotlieb

A Small Dragon

I've found a small dragon in the woodshed.
Think it must have come from deep inside a forest
because it's damp and green and leaves
are still reflecting in its eyes.

I fed it on many things, tried grass,
the roots of stars, hazel-nut and dandelion,
but it stared up at me as if to say, I need
foods you can't provide.

It made a nest among the coal,
not unlike a bird's but larger,
it is out of place here
and is quite silent.

If you believed in it I would come
hurrying to your house to let you share my wonder,
but I want instead to see
if you yourself will pass this way.

Brian Patten

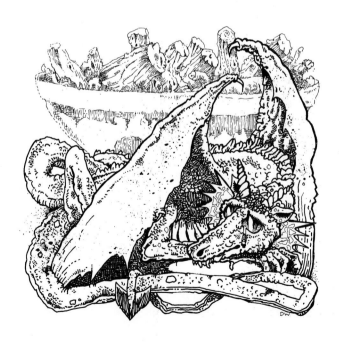

Fafnir

In the quiet waters
Of the forest pool
Fafnir the dragon
His tongue will cool

His tongue will cool
And his muzzle dip
Until the soft waters lave
His muzzle-tip

Happy the dragon
In the days expended
Before the time had come for dragons
To be hounded

Delivered in their simplicity
To the Knights of the Advancing Band
Who seeing the simple dragon
Must kill him out of hand.

When thy body shall be torn
And thy lofty spirit
Broken into pieces
For a Knight's merit,

When thy life-blood shall be spilt
And thy Being mild
In torment and dismay
To Death beguiled

Fafnir, I shall say then,
Thou art better dead
For the Knights have burnt thy grass
And thou couldst not have fed.

The time has not come yet
But must come soon
Meanwhile happy Fafnir
Take thy rest in the afternoon.

Take thy rest
Fafnir while thou mayest
In the long grass
Where thou liest

Happy knowing not
In thy simplicity
That the Knights have come
To do away with thee.

Stevie Smith

The Unicorn

The unicorn stood, like a king in a dream,
On the bank of a dark Senegambian stream;
And flaming flamingoes flew over his head,
As the African sun rose in purple and red.

Who knows what the thoughts of a unicorn are
When he shines on the world like a rising star;
When he comes from the magical pages of story
In the pride of his horn and a halo of glory?

He followed the paths where the jungle beasts go,
And he walked with a step that was stately and slow;
But he threw not a shadow and made not a sound,
And his foot was as light as the wind on the ground.

The lion looked up with his terrible eyes,
And growled like the thunder to hide his surprise.
He thought for a while, with a paw in the air;
Then tucked up his tail and turned into his lair.

The gentle giraffe ran away to relate
The news to his tawny and elegant mate,
While the snake slid aside with a venomous hiss,
And the little birds piped: 'There is something amiss!'

But the Unicorn strode with his head in a cloud
And uttered his innocent fancies aloud.
'What a wonderful world!' he was heard to exclaim;
'It is better than books: it is sweeter than fame!'

And he gazed at himself, with a thrill and a quiver,
Reflected in white by the slow-flowing river:
'O speak to me, dark Senegambian stream,
And prove that my beauty is more than a dream!'

He had paused for a word in the midst of his pride,
When a whisper came down through the leaves at his side
From a spying, malevolent imp of an ape
With a twist in his tail and a villainous shape:

'He was made by the stroke of a fanciful pen;
He was wholly invented by ignorant men.
One word in his ear, and one puff of the truth—
And a unicorn fades in the flower of his youth.'

The Unicorn heard, and the demon of doubt
Crept into his heart, and the sun was put out.
He looked in the water, but saw not a gleam
In the slow-flowing deep Senegambian stream.

He turned to the woods, and his shadowy form
Was seen through the trees like the moon in a storm.
And the darkness fell down on the Gambian plain;
And the stars of the Senegal sought him in vain.

He had come like a beautiful melody heard
When the strings of the fiddle are tunefully stirred;
And he passed where the splendours of melody go
When the hand of the fiddler surrenders the bow.

E. V. Rieu

Gluskap's Hound

They slew a god in a valley
    That faces the wooded west:
They held him down in their anger,
    With a mountain across his breast:
And all night through, and all night long,
    His hound will take no rest.

From low woods black as sorrow,
    That marshal along the lake,
A cry breaks out on the stillness
    As if the dead would wake—
The cry of Gluskap's hound, who hunts
    No more for hunting's sake,

But follows the sides of the valley,
    And the old, familiar trail,
With his nose to the ground, and his eyes
    Red lights in the cedar swale,
All night long and all night through,
    'Til the heavy east grows pale.

Some say he foreheralds tempest,
    Outrunning the wind in the air . . .
When willows are flying yellow
    And alders are wet and bare
He runs with no joy in the running,
    Giving tongue to his mad despair.

Another stick on the fire!
    The shadows are creeping near!
Something runs in the thicket
    The spruces droop to hear!
The black hound running in fierce despair,
    With his grief of a thousand year.

T. G. Roberts

A Rabbit as King of the Ghosts

The difficulty to think at the end of the day,
When the shapeless shadow covers the sun
And nothing is left except light on your fur—

There was the cat slopping its milk all day,
Fat cat, red tongue, green mind, white milk
And August the most peaceful month.

To be, in the grass, in the peacefullest time,
Without that monument of cat,
The cat forgotten in the moon;

And to feel that the light is a rabbit-light,
In which everything is meant for you
And nothing need be explained;

Then there is nothing to think of. It comes of itself;
And east rushes west and west rushes down,
No matter. The grass is full

And full of yourself. The trees around are for you,
The whole of the wideness of night is for you,
A self that touches all edges,

You become a self that fills the four corners of night.
The red cat hides away in the fur-light
And there you are humped high, humped up,

You are humped higher and higher, black as stone—
You sit with your head like a carving in space
And the little green cat is a bug in the grass.

Wallace Stevens

The Sea

The Sea

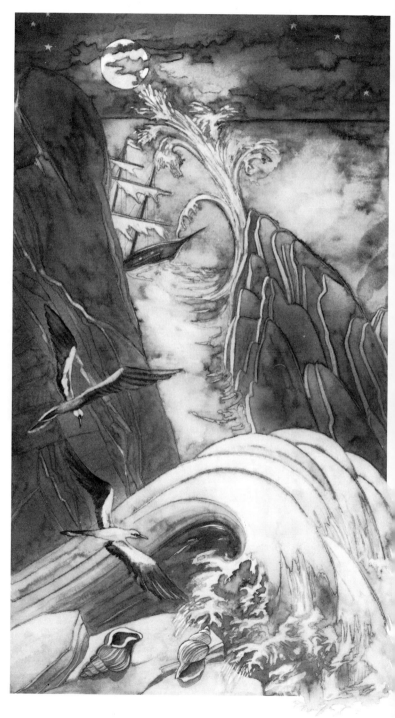

Frutta di Mare

I am a sea shell flung
Up from the ancient sea;
Now I lie here, among
Roots of a tamarisk tree;
No one listens to me.

I sing to myself all day
In a husky voice, quite low,
Things the great fishes say
And you must need to know;
All night I sing just so.

But lift me from the ground,
And hearken at my rim;
Only your sorrow's sound
Amazed, perplexed and dim,
Comes coiling to the brim;

For what the wise whales ponder
Awaking out from sleep,
The key to all your wonder,
The answers of the deep,
These to myself I keep.

Geoffrey Scott

The Shell

And then I pressed the shell
Close to my ear,
And listened well.
And straightway, like a bell,
Came low and clear
The slow, sad murmur of far distant seas
Whipped by an icy breeze
Upon a shore
Wind-swept and desolate.
It was a sunless strand that never bore
The footprint of a man,
Nor felt the weight

Since time began
Of any human quality or stir,
Save what the dreary winds and waves incur.
And in the hush of waters was the sound
Of pebbles, rolling round;
For ever rolling, with a hollow sound:
And bubbling sea-weeds, as the waters go,
Swish to and fro
Their long cold tentacles of slimy grey.
There was no day;
Nor ever came a night
Setting the stars alight
To wonder at the moon:
Was twilight only, and the frightened croon,
Smitten to whimpers, of the dreary wind
And waves that journeyed blind . . .
And then I loosed my ear—Oh, it was sweet
To hear a cart go jolting down the street.

James Stephens

Posted

Dream after dream I see the wrecks that lie
Unknown of man, unmarked upon the charts,
Known of the flat-fish with the withered eye,
And seen by women in their aching hearts.

World-wide the scattering is of those fair ships
That trod the billow tops till out of sight:
The cuttle mumbles them with horny lips,
The shells of the sea-insects crust them white.

In silence and in dimness and in greenness
Among the indistinct and leathery leaves
Of fruitless life they lie among the cleanness.
Fish glide and flit, slow under-movement heaves:

But no sound penetrates, not even the lunge
Of live ships passing, nor the gannet's plunge.

John Masefield

Little Fan

'I don't like the look of little Fan, mother,
    I don't like her looks a little bit.
Her face—well, it's not exactly different,
    But there's something wrong with it.

'She went down to the sea-shore yesterday,
    And she talked to somebody there,
Now she won't do anything but sit
    And comb out her yellowy hair.

'Her eyes are shiny and she sings, mother,
    Like nobody ever sang before.
Perhaps they gave her something queer to eat,
    Down by the rocks on the shore.

'Speak to me, speak, little Fan dear,
    Aren't you feeling very well?
Where have you been and what are you singing,
    And what's that seaweedy smell?

'Where did you get that shiny comb, love,
    And those pretty coral beads so red?
Yesterday you had two legs, I'm certain,
    But now there's something else instead.

'I don't like the looks of little Fan, mother,
    You'd best go and close the door.
Watch now, or she'll be gone for ever
    To the rocks by the brown sandy shore.'

James Reeves

They Call to One Another

They call to one another
 in the prisons of the sea
the mermen and mermaidens
 bound under lock and key
down in the green and salty dens
 and dungeons of the sea,
lying about in chains but
 dying to be free:
and this is why shortsighted men
 believe them not to be
for down to their dark dungeons it
 is very hard to see.

But sometimes morning fishermen
 drag up in the net
bits of bright glass or the silver comb
 of an old vanity set
or a letter rather hard to read
 because it is still wet
sent to remind us never, never
 never to forget

the mermen and mermaidens
 in the prisons of the sea
who call to one another
 when the stars of morning rise
and the stars of evening set
 for I have heard them calling
and I can hear them, yet.

George Barker

The Keeper of the Nore

My father he kept the Eddystone light
And he married a mer-mi-ade one night,
On account of which he had offspring three—
Two of them were fish and t'other was me.
When I was but a bit of a chip
I was put in charge of the Nore lightship:
I kept my lamps in very good style,
A-doing of the work according to Hoyle.

> Oh the rolling Nore, the raging Nore,
> The waves they tumble o'er and o'er;
> There's no such life to be had on shore,
> Like the life that is led by the man on the Nore.

One night as I was a-trimming of the glim,
A-singing a verse of the evening hymn,
I saw by the light of my signal lamp
The form of my mother looking awfully damp;
Just then a voice cries out 'Ahoy!'
And there she was a-sitting on a buoy—
That's a-meaning a buoy for the ships that sail,
And not a boy that's a juvenile male.

Says I to me mother, 'Now how do yer do?
And how's my father and my sisters two?'
Says she, 'It's an orph-i-an you are,
For you've only one sister, and you've got no pa.
Your father was drowned with several pals
And digested by the cannibals:
Of your sisters, one was cooked in a dish,
And t'other one is kept as a talking fish.'

At that I wept like a soft-eyed scamp—
My tears they made the water damp;
Says I to my mother, 'Won't you step within—
You look so wet—just to dry your skin?'
Says she, 'I likes the wet, my dear.'
Says I, 'Let me offer you the cabin chair.'
My mother, she looks at me with a frown,
'It's owing to my nature that I can't sit down.'

Says my mother, 'Now never you go on shore,
But always remain the man at the Nore.'
At that I saw a glittering scale,
And that was the end of my mother's tale.

Now, in deference to that maternal wish,
I can't visit my sister, the talking fish.
If you happen to see her when you go on shore,
Just give her the respects of the Man at the Nore.

Anon

.

The Wedding

Because there was no moon
our young sister was married
by the light of the stars.
She walked slowly the length
of the aisle of the river,
the stones arched above her
and the windows were water
patterned with lilies and garlands
    of reeds.
She walked with her bridegroom
down the nave of the sea
to the peal of the waves
and lightly-flung sand grains.
We called to her, called to her
and the echo returned to us
from the vaults of the ocean.
Because there was no moon
our young sister was married
by the light of the stars
and her heart was closed
within a light ring of coral.

Roland Gant

Deadman's Dirge

Prayer unsaid, and Mass unsung,
Deadman's dirge must still be rung:
    Dingle-dong, the dead-bells sound!
    Mermen chant his dirge around!

Wash him bloodless, smooth him fair,
Stretch his limbs, and sleek his hair:
    Dingle-dong, the dead-bells go!
    Mermen swing them to and fro!

In the wormless sand shall he
Feast for no foul gluttons be:
    Dingle-dong, the dead-bells chime!
    Mermen keep the tone and time!

We must with a tombstone brave
Shut the shark out from his grave:
    Dingle-dong, the dead-bells toll!
    Mermen dirgers ring his knoll!

Such a slab will we lay o'er him,
All the dead shall rise before him:
    Dingle-dong, the dead-bells boom!
    Mermen lay him in his tomb!

George Darley

Sea-change

Full fathom five thy father lies;
    Of his bones are coral made;
Those are pearls that were his eyes:
    Nothing of him that doth fade,
But doth suffer a sea-change
Into something rich and strange.
Sea-nymphs hourly ring his knell:
    Ding-dong.
Hark now I hear them, ding-dong bell.

William Shakespeare

The Kraken

Below the thunders of the upper deep;
Far, far beneath in the abysmal sea,
His ancient, dreamless, uninvaded sleep
The Kraken sleepeth: faintest sunlights flee
About his shadowy sides: above him swell
Huge sponges of millennial growth and height;
And far away into the sickly light,
From many a wondrous grot and secret cell
Unnumber'd and enormous polypi
Winnow with giant arms the slumbering green.
There hath he lain for ages and will lie
Battening upon huge seaworms in his sleep,
Until the latter fire shall heat the deep;
Then once by man and angels to be seen,
In roaring he shall rise and on the surface die.

Lord Tennyson

The Sea Serpant

An Accurate Description

A-sleepin' at length on the sand,
    Where the beach was all tidy and clean,
A-strokin' his scale with the brush on his tail
    The wily Sea Serpant I seen.

And what was his colour? you asks,
    And how did he look? inquires you,
I'll be busted and blessed if he didn't look jest
    Like you would of expected 'im to!

His head was the size of a—well,
    The size what they always attains;
He whistled a tune what was built like a prune,
    And his tail was the shape o' his brains.

His scales they was ruther—you know—
    Like the leaves what you pick off o' eggs;
And the way o' his walk—well, it's useless to talk,
    Fer o' course you've seen Sea Serpants' legs.

His length it was seventeen miles,
    Or fathoms, or inches, or feet
(Me memory's sich that I can't recall which,
    Though at figgers I've seldom been beat).

And I says as I looks at the beast,
    'He reminds me o' somethin' I've seen—
Is it candy or cats or humans or hats
    Or Fenimore Cooper I mean?'

And as I debated the point,
    In a way that I can't understand,
The Sea Serpant he disappeared in the sea
    And walked through the ocean by land.

And somehow I knowed he'd come back,
    So I marked off the place with me cap;
'Twas Lattitude West and Longtitude North
    And forty-eight cents by the map.

And his length it was seventeen miles,
    Or inches, or fathoms, or feet
    (Me memory's sich that I can't recall which,
    Though at figgers I've seldom been beat).

Wallace Irwin

The Sea Serpent
Chantey

There's a snake on the western wave
And his crest is red.
He is long as a city street,
And he eats the dead.
There's a hole in the bottom of the sea
Where the snake goes down.
And he waits in the bottom of the sea
For the men that drown.

Let the audience join
in the chorus
    This is the voice of the sand
    (The sailors understand)
  'There is far more sea than sand,
  There is far more sea than land.
  Yo . . . ho, yo . . . ho.'

He waits by the door of his cave
While the ages moan.
He cracks the ribs of the ships
With his teeth of stone.
In his gizzard deep and long
Much treasure lies.
Oh, the pearls and the Spanish gold ...
And the idols' eyes ...
Oh, the totem poles ... the skulls ...
The altars cold ...
The wedding rings, the dice ...
The buoy bells old.

    This is the voice of the sand
    (The sailors understand)
  'There is far more sea than sand,
  There is far more sea than land.
  Yo . . . ho, yo . . . ho.'

Dive, mermaids, with sharp swords
And cut him through,
And bring us the idols' eyes
And the red gold too.
Lower the grappling hooks
Good pirate men
And drag him up by the tongue
From his deep wet den.

We will sail to the end of the world,
We will nail his hide
To the mainmast of the moon
In the evening tide.

Or will you let him live,
The deep-sea thing,
With the wrecks of all the world
In a black wide ring
By the hole in the bottom of the sea
Where the snake goes down,
Where he waits in the bottom of the sea
For the men that drown?
    This is the voice of the sand
    (The sailors understand)
    'There is far more sea than sand,
    There is far more sea than land.
    Yo . . . ho, yo . . . ho.'

Vachel Lindsay

The *Alice Jean*

One moonlight night a ship drove in,
    A ghostly ship from the west,
Drifting with bare mast and lone tiller;
    Like a mermaid drest
In long green weed and barnacles
    She beached and came to rest.

All the watchers of the coast
    Flocked to view the sight;
Men and women, streaming down
    Through the summer night,
Found her standing tall and ragged
    Beached in the moonlight.

Then one old woman stared aghast:
    'The *Alice Jean*? But no!
The ship that took my Ned from me
    Sixty years ago—
Drifted back from the utmost west
    With the ocean's flow?

89

'Caught and caged in the weedy pool
    Beyond the western brink,
Where crewless vessels lie and rot
    In waters black as ink,
Torn out at last by a sudden gale—
    Is it the *Jean*, you think?'

A hundred women gaped at her,
    The menfolk nudged and laughed,
But none could find a likelier story
    For the strange craft
With fear and death and desolation
    Rigged fore and aft.

The blind ship came forgotten home
    To all but one of these,
Of whom none dared to climb aboard her:
    And by and by the breeze
Veered hard about, and the *Alice Jean*
    Foundered in foaming seas.

Robert Graves

Music

Chamber Music

Lean out of the window,
    Goldenhair,
I hear you singing
    A merry air.

My book is closed,
    I read no more,
Watching the fire dance
    On the floor.

I have left my book:
    I have left my room:
For I heard you singing
    Through the gloom,

Singing and singing
    A merry air.
Lean out of the window,
    Goldenhair.

James Joyce

The Music of the Island

Be not afeard; the isle is full of noises,
Sounds and sweet airs, that give delight, and hurt not.
Sometimes a thousand twangling instruments
Will hum about mine ears; and sometimes voices,
That, if I then had wak'd after long sleep,
Will make me sleep again: and then, in dreaming,
The clouds methought would open, and show riches
Ready to drop upon me; that, when I wak'd,
I cried to dream again.

William Shakespeare

The Splendour Falls on Castle Walls

The splendour falls on castle walls
    And snowy summits old in story:
The long light shakes across the lakes,
    And the wild cataract leaps in glory.
Blow, bugle, blow, set the wild echoes flying,
Blow, bugle; answer, echoes, dying, dying, dying.

O hark, O hear! how thin and clear,
    And thinner, clearer, farther going!
O sweet and far from cliff and scar
    The horns of Elfland faintly blowing!
Blow, let us hear the purple glens replying:
Blow, bugle; answer, echoes, dying, dying, dying.

O love, they die in yon rich sky,
    They faint on hill or field or river:
Our echoes roll from soul to soul,
    And grow for ever and for ever.
Blow, bugle, blow, set the wild echoes flying,
And answer, echoes, answer, dying, dying, dying.

Lord Tennyson

A Musical Instrument

What was he doing, the great god Pan,
Down in the reeds by the river?
Spreading ruin and scattering ban,
Splashing and paddling with hoofs of a goat,
And breaking the golden lilies afloat
With the dragon-fly on the river.

He tore out a reed, the great god Pan,
From the deep cool bed of the river;
The limpid water turbidly ran,
And the broken lilies a-dying lay,
And the dragon-fly had fled away,
Ere he brought it out of the river.

High on the shore sat the great god Pan,
While turbidly flow'd the river;
And hack'd and hew'd as a great god can
With his hard bleak steel at the patient reed,
Till there was not a sign of the leaf indeed
To prove it fresh from the river.

He cut it short, did the great god Pan
(How tall it grew in the river!)
Then drew the pith, like the heart of a man,
Steadily, from the outside ring,
And notch'd the poor dry empty thing
In holes, as he sat by the river.

'This is the way,' laugh'd the great god Pan
(Laugh'd while he sat by the river),
'The only way, since gods began
To make sweet music, they could succeed.'
Then dropping his mouth to a hole in the reed,
He blew in power by the river.

Sweet, sweet, sweet, O Pan!
Piercing sweet by the river!
Blinding sweet, O great god Pan!
The sun on the hill forgot to die,
And the lilies revived, and the dragon-fly
Came back to dream on the river.

Yet half a beast is the great god Pan,
To laugh as he sits by the river,
Making a poet out of a man :
The true gods sigh for the cost and pain—
For the reed which grows nevermore again
As a reed with the reeds of the river.

Elizabeth Barrett Browning

The Singing Cat

It was a little captive cat
    Upon a crowded train
His mistress takes him from his box
    To ease his fret and pain.

She holds him tight upon her knee
    The graceful animal
And all the people look at him
    He is so beautiful.

But oh he pricks and oh he prods
    And turns upon her knee
Then lifteth up his innocent voice
    In plaintive melody.

He lifteth up his innocent voice
    He lifteth up, he singeth
And to each human countenance
    A smile of grace he bringeth.

He lifteth up his innocent paw
    Upon her breast he clingeth
And everybody cries, Behold
    The cat, the cat that singeth.

He lifteth up his innocent voice
    He lifteth up, he singeth
And all the people warm themselves
    In the love his beauty bringeth.

Stevie Smith

Narnian Suite

March for Strings, Kettledrums, and Sixty-three Dwarfs

With plucking pizzicato and the prattle of the kettledrum
We're trotting into battle mid a clatter of accoutrement;
Our beards are big as periwigs and trickle with opopanax,
And trinketry and treasure twinkle out on every part of us—
    (Scrape! Tap! The fiddle and the kettledrum).

The chuckle-headed humans think we're only petty poppetry
And all our battle-tackle nothing more than pretty bric-a-
                              brac;
But a little shrub has prickles, and they'll soon be in a
                          pickle if
A scud of dwarfish archery has crippled all their cavalry—
    (Whizz! Twang! The quarrel and the javelin).

And when the tussle thickens we can writhe and wriggle
                          under it;
Then dagger-point'll tickle 'em, and grab and grip'll
                          grapple 'em,
And trap and trick'll trouble 'em and tackle 'em and
                          topple 'em
Till they're huddled, all be-diddled, in the middle of
                          our caperings—
    (Dodge! Jump! The wriggle and the summersault).

When we've scattered 'em and peppered 'em with pebbles from
   our catapults
We'll turn again in triumph and by crannies and by crevices
Go back to where the capitol and cradle of our people is,
Our forges and our furnaces, the caverns of the earth—
    (Gold! Fire! The anvil and the smithying).

March for Drum, Trumpet, and Twenty-one Giants

With stumping stride in pomp and pride
We come to thump and floor ye;
We'll bump your lumpish heads today
And tramp your ramparts into clay,
And as we stamp and romp and play
Our trump'll blow before us—
endo)   Oh tramp it, tramp it, tramp it, trumpet,
       trumpet blow before us!

We'll grind and break and bind and take
And plunder ye and pound ye!
With trundled rocks and bludgeon blow,
You dunderheads, we'll dint ye so
You'll blunder and run blind, as though
By thunder stunned, around us—
By thunder, thunder, thunder, thunder stunned around us!

Ho! tremble town and tumble down
And crumble shield and sabre!
Your kings will mumble and look pale,
Your horses stumble or turn tail,
Your skimble-scamble counsels fail,
So rumble drum belaboured—
diminuendo) Oh rumble, rumble, rumble, rumble, rumble
        drum belaboured!

C. S. Lewis

The Aim was Song

Before man came to blow it right
    The wind once blew itself untaught,
And did its loudest day and night
    In any rough place where it caught.

Man came to tell it what was wrong:
    It hadn't found the place to blow;
It blew too hard—the aim was song.
    And listen—how it ought to go!

He took a little in his mouth,
    And held it long enough for north
To be converted into south,
    And then by measure blew it forth.

By measure. It was word and note,
    The wind the wind had meant to be—
A little through the lips and throat.
    The aim was song—the wind could see.

Robert Frost

98

The Moon and Stars

The
Moon
and
Stars

Star-talk

'Are you awake, Gemelli,
    This frosty night?'
'We'll be awake till reveille,
 Which is Sunrise,' say the Gemelli,
'It's no good trying to go to sleep:
 If there's wine to be got we'll drink it deep,
    But sleep is gone for tonight,
    But sleep is gone for tonight.'

'Are you cold too, poor Pleiads,
    This frosty night?'
'Yes, and so are the Hyads:
 See us cuddle and hug,' say the Pleiads,
'All six in a ring: it keeps us warm:
 We huddle together like birds in a storm:
    It's bitter weather tonight,
    It's bitter weather tonight.'

'What do you hunt, Orion,
    This starry night?'
'The Ram, the Bull and the Lion,
 And the Great Bear,' says Orion,
'With my starry quiver and beautiful belt
 I am trying to find a good thick pelt
    To warm my shoulders tonight,
    To warm my shoulders tonight.'

'Did you hear that, Great She-bear,
    This frosty night?'
'Yes, he's talking of stripping *me* bare,
 Of my own big fur,' says the She-bear.
'I'm afraid of the man and his terrible arrow:
 The thought of it chills my bones to the marrow,
    And the frost so cruel tonight!
    And the frost so cruel tonight!'

'How is your trade, Aquarius,
    This frosty night?'
'Complaints is many and various,
 And my feet are cold,' says Aquarius,
'There's Venus objects to the Dolphin-scales,
 And Mars to Crab-spawn found in my pails,
    And the pump has frozen tonight,
    And the pump has frozen tonight.'

Robert Graves   101

Canis Major

The great Overdog.
That heavenly beast
With a star in one eye,
Gives a leap in the east.

He dances upright
All the way to the west
And never once drops
On his forefeet to rest.

I'm a poor underdog,
But tonight I will bark
With the great Overdog
That romps through the dark.

Robert Frost

who knows if the moon's

who knows if the moon's
a balloon, coming out of a keen city
in the sky—filled with pretty people?
(and if you and i should

get into it, if they
should take me and take you into their balloon,
why then
we'd go up higher with all the pretty people

than houses and steeples and clouds:
go sailing
away and away sailing into a keen
city which nobody's ever visited, where

always
          it's
               Spring) and everyone's
in love and flowers pick themselves

e.e. cummings

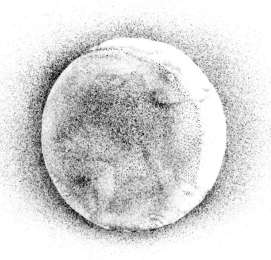

Full Moon Rhyme

There's a hare in the moon tonight,
crouching alone in the bright
buttercup field of the moon;
and all the dogs in the world
howl at the hare in the moon.

'I chased that hare to the sky,'
the hungry dogs all cry.
'The hare jumped into the moon
and left me here in the cold.
I chased that hare to the moon.'

'Come down again, mad hare.
We can see you there,'
the dogs all howl to the moon.
'Come down again to the world,
you mad black hare in the moon,

or we will grow wings and fly
up to the star-grassed sky
to hunt you out of the moon,'
the hungry dogs of the world
howl at the hare in the moon.

Judith Wright

The Cat and the Moon

The cat went here and there
And the moon spun round like a top,
And the nearest kin of the moon,
The creeping cat, looked up.
Black Minnaloushe stared at the moon,
For, wander and wail as he would,
The pure cold light in the sky
Troubled his animal blood.
Minnaloushe runs in the grass
Lifting his delicate feet.
Do you dance, Minnaloushe, do you dance?
When two close kindred meet,
What better than call a dance?
Maybe the moon may learn,
Tired of that courtly fashion,
A new dance turn.
Minnaloushe creeps through the grass
From moonlit place to place,
The sacred moon overhead
Has taken a new phase.
Does Minnaloushe know that his pupils
Will pass from change to change,
And that from round to crescent,
From crescent to round they range?
Minnaloushe creeps through the grass
Alone, important and wise,
And lifts to the changing moon
His changing eyes.

W. B. Yeats

Silver

Slowly, silently, now the moon
Walks the night in her silver shoon;
This way, and that, she peers, and sees
Silver fruit upon silver trees;
One by one the casements catch
Her beams beneath the silvery thatch;
Couched in his kennel like a log,
With paws of silver sleeps the dog;
From their shadowy cote the white breasts peep
Of doves in a silver-feathered sleep;
The harvest mouse goes scampering by,
With silver claws, and silver eye;
And moveless fish in the water gleam,
By silver reeds in a silver stream.

Walter de la Mare

Moon-Whales

They plough through the moon-stuff
Just under the surface
Lifting the moon's skin
Like a muscle
But so slowly it seems like a lasting mountain
Breathing so rarely it seems like a volcano
Leaving a hole blasted in the moon's skin

Sometimes they plunge deep
Under the moon's plains
Making their magnetic way
Through the moon's interior metals
Sending the astronaut's instruments scatty

Their music is immense
Each note hundreds of years long
Each complete tune a moon-age

So they sing to each other unending songs
As unmoving they move their immovable masses

Their eyes closed ecstatic

Ted Hughes

Foxgloves

Foxgloves on the moon keep to dark caves.
They come out at the dark of the moon only and in waves
Swarm through the moon-towns and wherever there's a chink
Slip into the houses and spill all the money, clink-clink,
And crumple the notes and re-arrange the silver dishes,
And dip hands into the goldfish bowls and stir the goldfishes,
And thumb the edges of mirrors, and touch the sleepers
Then at once vanish into the far distance with a wild laugh
　　leaving the house smelling faintly of Virginia Creepers.

Ted Hughes

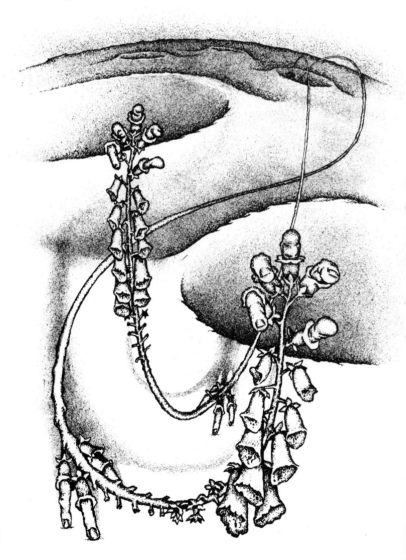

The Spirit of
the Place

The Spirit of the Place

The Path

Running along a bank, a parapet
That saves from the precipitous wood below
The level road, there is a path. It serves
Children for looking down the long smooth steep,
Between the legs of beech and yew, to where
A fallen tree checks the sight: while men and women
Content themselves with the road and what they see
Over the bank, and what the children tell.
The path, winding like silver, trickles on,
Bordered and even invaded by thinnest moss
That tries to cover roots and crumbling chalk
With gold, olive, and emerald, but in vain.
The children wear it. They have flattened the bank
On top, and silvered it between the moss
With the current of their feet, year after year.
But the road is houseless, and leads not to school.
To see a child is rare there, and the eye
Has but the road, the wood that overhangs
And underyawns it, and the path that looks
As if it led on to some legendary
Or fancied place where men have wished to go
And stay; till, sudden, it ends where the wood ends.

Edward Thomas

The Way Through the Woods

They shut the road through the woods
Seventy years ago.
Weather and rain have undone it again,
And now you would never know
There was once a road through the woods
Before they planted the trees.
It is underneath the coppice and heath,
And the thin anemones.
Only the keeper sees
That, where the ring-dove broods,
And the badgers roll at ease,
There was once a road through the woods.

Yet, if you enter the woods
Of a summer evening late,
When the night-air cools on the trout-ringed pools
Where the otter whistles his mate,
(They fear not men in the woods,
Because they see so few),
You will hear the beat of a horse's feet,
And the swish of a skirt in the dew,
Steadily cantering through
The misty solitudes,
As though they perfectly knew
The old lost road through the woods . . .
But there is no road through the woods.

Rudyard Kipling

The Toadstool Wood

The toadstool wood is dark and mouldy,
    And has a ferny smell.
About the trees hangs something quiet
    And queer—like a spell.

Beneath the arching sprays of bramble
    Small creatures make their holes;
Over the moss's close green velvet
    The stilted spider strolls.

The stalks of toadstools pale and slender
    That grow from that old log,
Bars they might be to imprison
    A prince turned to a frog.

There lives no mumbling witch nor wizard
    In this uncanny place,
Yet you might think you saw at twilight
    A small, crafty face.

James Reeves

Evening

Of an evening, Mrs Kembley
Would wait for Mr Kembley on the hill—
Waiting a little frightened,
For the woods under were so still,
                              So still,
For the mist crept up the nearer valleys,
Whispering white and chill;
Down in them something murmured,
    (Was it the distant rill?)
More dusky grew the long green alleys,
And the voices of the woods stabbed, sharp and
                              shrill.
Then the nearest light winked yonder,
    Miles down, by the mill,
And the Roman road ran straight and silent,
Empty and waiting, it seemed, along the hill.

She knew there was no reason to be frightened,
There was nothing for her to fear.
The valleys thus were always whitened
By the mist; the cruel wood voices sounded shrill
Always when all else was still—
But darkness was sidling near,
                              And nearer,
And Mrs Kembley waited on the hill . . .

Osbert Sitwell

Landscape as Werewolf

Near here, the last grey wolf
In England was clubbed down. Still,
After two hundred years, the same pinched wind
Rakes through his cairn of bones

As he squats quiet, watching daylight seep
Away from the scarred granite, and its going drain
The hills' bare faces. Far below,
A tiny bus twists on its stringy path
And scuttles home around a darkening bend.

The fells contract, regroup in starker forms;
Dusk tightens on them, as the wind gets up
And stretches hungrily: tensed at the nape,
The coarse heath bristles like a living pelt.

The sheep are all penned in. Down at the pub
They sing, and shuttle darts: the hostellers
Dubbin their heavy boots. Above the crags
The first stars prick their eyes and bide their time.

William Dunlop

The Wind was on the Withered Heath

The wind was on the withered heath,
but in the forest stirred no leaf:
there shadows lay by night and day,
and dark things silent crept beneath.

The wind came down from mountains cold,
and like a tide it roared and rolled;
the branches groaned, the forest moaned,
and leaves were laid upon the mould.

The wind went on from West to East;
all movement in the forest ceased,
but shrill and harsh across the marsh
its whistling voices were released.

The grasses hissed, their tassels bent,
the reeds were rattling—on it went
o'er shaken pool under heavens cool
where racing clouds were torn and rent.

It passed the lonely Mountain bare
and swept above the dragon's lair:
there black and dark lay boulders stark
and flying smoke was in the air.

It left the world and took its flight
over the wide seas of the night.
The moon set sail upon the gale,
and stars were fanned to leaping might.

J. R. R. Tolkien   113

John Polruddon

John Polruddon
All of a sudden
Went out of his house one night,

      When a privateer
      Came sailing near
      Under his window-light.

They saw his jugs
His plates and his mugs
His hearth as bright as brass,

      His gews and gaws
      And kicks and shaws
      All through their spying-glass.

They saw his wine
His silver shine
They heard his fiddlers play.

      Tonight, they said,
      Out of his bed
      Polruddon we'll take away.

And from a skiff
They climbed the cliff
And crossed the salt-wet lawn,

      And as they crept
      Polruddon slept
      The night away to dawn.

In air or ground
What is that sound?
Polruddon said, and stirred.

      They breathed, Be still,
      It was the shrill
      Of the scritch-owl you heard.

O yet again
I hear it plain,
But do I wake or dream?

      In morning's fog
      The otter-dog
      Is whistling by the stream,

Now from the sea
What comes for me
Beneath my window dark?

Lie still, my dear,
All that you hear
Is the red fox's bark.

Swift from his bed
Polruddon was sped
Before the day was white,

And head and feet
Wrapped in a sheet
They bore him down the height.

And never more
Through his own door
Polruddon went nor came,

Though many a tide
Has turned beside
The cliff that bears his name.

On stone and brick
Was ivy thick
And the grey roof was thin,

And winter's gale
With fists of hail
Broke all the windows in.

The chimney-crown
It tumbled down
And up grew the green,

Till on the cliff
It was as if
A house had never been.

But when the moon
Swims late or soon
Across St Austell Bay,

What sight, what sound
Haunts air and ground
Where once Polruddon lay?

It is the high
White scritch-owl's cry
The fox as dark as blood,

And on the hill
The otter still
Whistles beside the flood.

Charles Causley

Journeys and Struggles

from Tom of Bedlam's Song

From the hag and hungry goblin
That into rags would rend ye,
All the spirits that stand
By the naked man
In the book of moons, defend ye.

That of your five sound senses
You never be forsaken,
Nor wander from
Yourselves with Tom
Abroad to beg your bacon.

The moon's my constant mistress,
And the lonely owl my marrow;
The flaming drake
And the night-crow make
Me music to my sorrow.

With an host of furious fancies,
Whereof I am commander,
With a burning spear
And a horse of air
To the wilderness I wander;

By a knight of ghost and shadows
I summoned am to tourney
Ten leagues beyond
The wide world's end—
Methinks it is no journey.

Anon

The Song of Wandering Aengus

I went out to the hazel wood,
Because a fire was in my head,
And cut and peeled a hazel wand,
And hooked a berry to a thread;
And when white moths were on the wing,
And moth-like stars were flickering out,
I dropped the berry in a stream
And caught a little silver trout.

When I had laid it on the floor
I went to blow the fire aflame,
But something rustled on the floor,
And some one called me by my name:
It had become a glimmering girl
With apple blossom in her hair
Who called me by my name and ran
And faded through the brightening air.

Though I am old with wandering
Through hollow lands and hilly lands,
I will find out where she has gone,
And kiss her lips and take her hands;
And walk among long dappled grass,
And pluck till time and times are done
The silver apples of the moon,
The golden apples of the sun.

W. B. Yeats

Romance

When I was but thirteen or so
    I went into a golden land,
Chimborazo, Cotopaxi
    Took me by the hand.

My father died, my brother too,
    They passed like fleeting dreams.
I stood where Popocatapetl
    In the sunlight gleams.

I dimly heard the Master's voice
    And boys far-off at play,
Chimborazo, Cotopaxi
    Had stolen me away.

I walked in a great golden dream
    To and fro from school—
Shining Popocatapetl
    The dusty streets did rule.

I walked home with a gold dark boy
    And never a word I'd say,
Chimborazo, Cotopaxi
    Had taken my speech away:

I gazed entranced upon his face
    Fairer than any flower—
O shining Popocatapetl
    It was thy magic hour:

The houses, people, traffic seemed
    Thin fading dreams by day,
Chimborazo, Cotopaxi
    They had stolen my soul away!

Walter James Turner

Song from 'Mirage'

(Sung to a guitar by 'a young favourite Kurd,
a mongrel child of the bazaar, whose voice was like
a singing bird')

I know a Room where tulips tall
    And almond-blossom pale
Are coloured on the frescoed wall.

I know a River where the ships
    Drift by with ghostly sail
And dead men chant with merry lips.

I know the Garden by the sea
    Where birds with painted wings
Mottle the dark magnolia Tree.

I know the never-failing Source,
    I know the Bush that sings,
The Vale of Gems, the flying Horse,

I know the Dog that was a Prince,
    The talking Nightingale,
The Hill of glass, the magic Quince,

I know the lovely Lake of Van;
    Yet, knowing all these things,
        I wander with a caravan,
        I wander with a caravan!

V. Sackville-West

Eldorado

Gaily bedight,
A gallant knight,
In sunshine and in shadow,
Had journeyed long,
Singing a song,
In search of Eldorado.

But he grew old—
This knight so bold—
And o'er his heart a shadow
Fell as he found
No spot of ground
That looked like Eldorado.

And, as his strength
Failed him at length,
He met a pilgrim shadow—
'Shadow,' said he,
'Where can it be—
This land of Eldorado?'

'Over the Mountains
Of the Moon,
Down the Valley of the Shadow,
Ride, boldly ride,'
The shade replied,—
'If you seek for Eldorado!'

Edgar Allan Poe

Jabberwocky

'Twas brillig, and the slithy toves
　　Did gyre and gimble in the wabe;
All mimsy were the borogoves,
　　And the mome raths outgrabe.

'Beware the Jabberwock, my son!
　　The jaws that bite, the claws that catch!
Beware the Jubjub bird, and shun
　　The frumious Bandersnatch!'

He took his vorpal sword in hand:
　　Long time the manxome foe he sought—
So rested he by the Tumtum tree,
　　And stood awhile in thought.

And as in uffish thought he stood,
　　The Jabberwock, with eyes of flame,
Came whiffling through the tulgey wood,
　　And burbled as it came!

One, two! One, two! And through and through
　　The vorpal blade went snicker-snack!
He left it dead, and with its head
　　He went galumphing back.

'And hast thou slain the Jabberwock?
　　Come to my arms, my beamish boy!
O frabjous day! Callooh! Callay!'
　　He chortled in his joy.

'Twas brillig, and the slithy toves
　　Did gyre and gimble in the wabe;
All mimsy were the borogoves,
　　And the mome raths outgrabe.

Lewis Carroll

The Lambton Worm

Whisht lads, haud your gobs
I'll tell yez all an awful story
Whisht lads, haud your gobs
I'll tell ye 'boot the worm.

One Sunday morning Lambton went
A-fishing in the Wear
And catched a fish upon his hook
He thowt looked varry queer
But whatna kind of fish it was
Young Lambton couldn't tell
He wouldn't fash to carry it hyem
So he hoyed it doon a well.

Now Lambton felt inclined to gan
And fight in foreign wars
He joined a troop of knights that cared
For neither wounds nor scars
And off he went to Palestine
Where queer things him befell
And varry soon forgot aboot
The queer worm doon the well.

Now this worm got fat and growed and growed
And growed an awful size
Wi' greet big head and greet big gob
And greet big goggly eyes
And when, at neets, he crawled aboot
To pick up bits of news
If he felt dry upon the road
He milked a dozen coos.

This awful worm would often feed
On calves and lambs and sheep
And swellied little bairns alive
When they lay doon to sleep.
And when he'd eaten all he could
And he had had his fill
He crawled away and lapped his tail
Ten times round Penshaw hill.

Now news of this most awful worm
And his queer gannins-on
Soon crossed the seas, got to the ears
Of brave and bold Sir John.
So hyem he come and he catched the beast
And cut it in three halves
And that soon stopped his eating bairns
And sheep and lambs and calves.

Now lads I'll haud me gob
That's all I know aboot the story
Of Sir John's clever job
Wi' the famous Lambton Worm.

Anon

Adventures of Isabel

Isabel met an enormous bear,
Isabel, Isabel, didn't care;
The bear was hungry, the bear was ravenous,
The bear's big mouth was cruel and cavernous.
The bear said, Isabel, glad to meet you,
How do, Isabel, now I'll eat you!
Isabel, Isabel, didn't worry,
Isabel didn't scream or scurry.
She washed her hands and she straightened her hair up
Then Isabel quietly ate the bear up.

Once in a night as black as pitch
Isabel met a wicked old witch.
The witch's face was cross and wrinkled,
The witch's gums with teeth were sprinkled.
Ho ho, Isabel! the old witch crowed,
I'll turn you into an ugly toad!
Isabel, Isabel, didn't worry,
Isabel didn't scream or scurry,
She showed no rage and she showed no rancour,
But she turned the witch into milk and drank her.

Isabel met a hideous giant,
Isabel continued self-reliant.
The giant was hairy, the giant was horrid,
He had one eye in the middle of his forehead.
Good morning, Isabel, the giant said,
I'll grind your bones to make my bread.
Isabel, Isabel, didn't worry,
Isabel didn't scream or scurry.
She nibbled the zwieback that she always fed off,
And when it was gone, she cut the giant's head off.

Ogden Nash

Two Songs of the Dwarves:

Far Over the Misty Mountains

Far over the misty mountains cold
To dungeons deep and caverns old
We must away ere break of day
To seek the pale enchanted gold.

The dwarves of yore made mighty spells,
While hammers fell like ringing bells
In places deep, where dark things sleep,
In hollow halls beneath the fells.

For ancient king and elvish lord
There many a gleaming golden hoard
They shaped and wrought, and light they caught
To hide in gems on hilt of sword.

On silver necklaces they strung
The flowering stars, on crowns they hung
The dragon-fire, in twisted wire
They meshed the light of moon and sun.

Far over the misty mountains cold
To dungeons deep and caverns old
We must away, ere break of day,
To claim our long-forgotten gold.

Goblets they carved there for themselves
And harps of gold; where no man delves
There lay they long, and many a song
Was sung unheard by men or elves.

The pines were roaring on the height,
The winds were moaning in the night.
The fire was red, it flaming spread;
The trees like torches blazed with light.

The bells were ringing in the dale
And men looked up with faces pale;
The dragon's ire more fierce than fire
Laid low their towers and houses frail.

The mountains smoked beneath the moon;
The dwarves, they heard the tramp of doom.
They fled their hall to dying fall
Beneath his feet, beneath the moon.

Far over the misty mountains grim
To dungeons deep and caverns dim
We must away, ere break of day,
To win our harps and gold from him!

J. R. R. Tolkien

Under the Mountain
Dark and Tall

Under the Mountain dark and tall
The King has come unto his hall!
His foe is dead, the Worm of Dread,
And ever so his foes shall fall.

The sword is sharp, the spear is long,
The arrow swift, the Gate is strong;
The heart is bold that looks on gold;
The dwarves no more shall suffer wrong.

The dwarves of yore made mighty spells,
While hammers fell like ringing bells
In places deep, where dark things sleep,
In hollow halls beneath the fells.

On silver necklaces they strung
The light of stars, on crowns they hung
The dragon-fire, from twisted wire
The melody of harps they wrung.

The mountain throng once more is freed!
O! wandering folk, the summons heed!
Come haste! Come haste! across the waste!
The king of friend and kin has need.

Now call we over mountains cold,
'Come back unto the caverns old!'
Here at the Gates the king awaits,
His hands are rich with gems and gold.

The king is come unto his hall
Under the Mountain dark and tall.
The Worm of Dread is slain and dead,
And ever so our foes shall fall!

J. R. R. Tolkien

Sir Eglamour

Sir Eglamour, that worthy knight,
He took his sword and went to fight;
And as he rode both hill and dale,
Armèd upon his shirt of mail,
A dragon came out of his den,
Had slain, God knows how many men!

When he espied Sir Eglamour,
Oh, if you had but heard him roar,
And seen how all the trees did shake,
The knight did tremble, horse did quake,
The birds betake them all to peeping—
It would have made you fall a weeping!

But now it is in vain to fear,
Being come unto, 'fight dog! fight bear!'
To it they go and fiercely fight
A live-long day from morn till night.
The dragon had a plaguy hide,
And could the sharpest steel abide.

No sword will enter him with cuts,
Which vexed the knight unto the guts;
But, as in choler he did burn,
He watched the dragon a good turn;
And, as a-yawning he did fall,
He thrust his sword in, hilts and all.

Then, like a coward, he did fly
Unto his den that was hard by;
And there he lay all night and roared.
The knight was sorry for his sword,
But, riding thence, said, 'I forsake it,
He that will fetch it, let him take it!'

Samuel Rowlands

Magicians and Devils

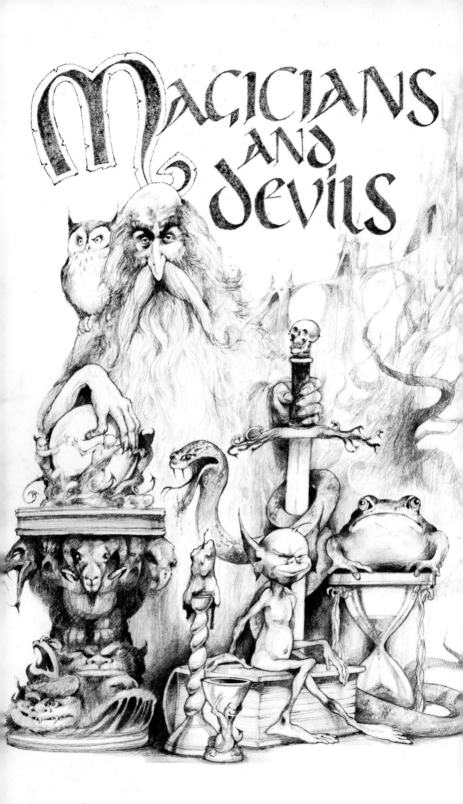

Magicians and Devils

Alone in the Grange

Strange,
Strange,
Is the little old man
Who lives in the Grange.
Old,
Old;
And they say that he keeps
A box full of gold.
Bowed,
Bowed,
Is his thin little back
That once was so proud.
Soft,
Soft,
Are his steps as he climbs
The stairs to the loft.
Black,
Black,
Is the old shuttered house.
Does he sleep on a sack?

They say he does magic,
That he can cast spells,
That he prowls round the garden
Listening for bells;
That he watches for strangers,
Hates every soul,
And peers with his dark eye
Through the keyhole.

I wonder, I wonder,
As I lie in my bed,
Whether he sleeps with his hat on his head?
Is he really magician
With altar of stone
Or a lonely old gentleman
Left on his own?

Gregory Harrison

The Magician's Attic

The woodwork's musty as the russet smell of
    old burnt toast and almonds.
The feather-hands
Of the falcon-clock have stopped.
          There are no sounds,
Except the old creaking rocking-throne that
    stands
In a corner (still rocking, for kings and queens
    have ghosts called Histories).
          Ends
Of cowboys' cattle-brands
Hang on a wall.
          The table's one leg bends
Like a toad-stool stalk.
          The magician never mends
His old things. He never sends
Them to auction-sales, bazaars or jumble-
    sales. Indeed, he intends
To keep his attic cluttered with peaceful
      rubbish
    quieter than islands.
The air is still with the dust of grated
    diamonds.
The feather-hands
Of the falcon-clock have stopped.
          He finds

Old things are good for games of memories,
   and sometimes he stands
For hours staring at wands—
For this is where he keeps them, old,
   splintered, broken, worn-out wizard wands.

Harold Massingham

The Hag

The Hag is astride,
This night for to ride;
The Devil and she together:
   Through thick and through thin,
   Now out and then in,
Though n'er so foul be the weather.

A thorn or a burr
She takes for a spur:
With a lash of a bramble she rides now,
   Through brakes and through briers,
   O'er ditches and mires,
She follows the Spirit that guides now.

No beast, for his food.
Dares now range the wood;
But hushed in his lair he lies lurking:
   While mischiefs, by these,
   On land and on seas,
At noon of night are a-working.

The storm will arise
And trouble the skies;
This night, and more for the wonder,
   The ghost from the tomb
   Affrighted shall come,
Called out by the clap of the thunder.

Robert Herrick

Witches' Charms

Dame, dame! the watch is set:
Quickly come, we all are met.
From the lakes and from the fens,
From the rocks and from the dens,
From the woods and from the caves,
From the churchyards, from the graves,
From the dungeon, from the tree
That they die on, here are we!

      Comes she not yet?
      Strike another heat!

The weather is fair, the wind is good:
Up, dame, on your horse of wood!
Or else tuck up your grey frock,
And saddle your goat or your green cock,
And make his bridle a ball of thread
To roll up how many miles you have rid.
Quickly come away,
For we all stay.

      Not yet? nay then
      We'll try her again.

The owl is abroad, the bat, and the toad,
    And so is the cat-a-mountain,
The ant, and the mole sit both in a hole,
    And frog peeps out o' the fountain;
The dogs they do bay, and the timbrels play,
    The spindle is now a-turning;
The moon it is red, and the stars are fled,
    But all the sky is a-burning:
The ditch is made, and our nails the spade,
With pictures full, of wax and of wool;
Their livers I stick with needles quick;
There lacks but the blood to make up the flood.
    Quickly, Dame, then, bring your part in!
Spur, spur upon little Martin!
Merrily, merrily, make him sail,
A worm in his mouth, and a thorn in's tail,

Fire above, and fire below,
With a whip i' your hand, to make him go!

O now she's come
Let all be dumb.

Ben Jonson

Two Witches

There was a witch
The witch had an itch
The itch was so itchy it
Gave her a twitch.

Another witch
Admired the twitch
So she started twitching
Though she had no itch.

Now both of them twitch
So it's hard to tell which
Witch has the itch and
Which witch has the twitch.

Alexander Resnikoff

The Witch's Cat

'My magic is dead,' said the witch. 'I'm astounded
That people can fly to the moon and around it.
It used to be mine and the cat's till they found it.
My broomstick is draughty, I snivel with cold
As I ride to the stars. I'm painfully old,
     And so is my cat;
     But planet-and-space-ship,
     Rocket or race-ship
Never shall part me from that.'

She wrote an advertisement, 'Witch in a fix
Willing to part with the whole bag of tricks,
Going cheap at the price at eighteen and six.'
But no one was ready to empty his coffers
For out-of-date rubbish. There weren't any offers—
     Except for the cat.
     'But planet-and-space-ship,
     Rocket or race-ship
Never shall part me from that.'

The tears trickled fast, not a sentence she spoke
As she stamped on her broom and the brittle stick broke,
And she dumped in a dustbin her hat and her cloak,
Then clean disappeared, leaving no prints;
And no one at all has set eyes on her since
     Or her tired old cat.
     'But planet-and-space-ship,
     Rocket or race-ship
Never shall part me from that.'

Ian Serraillier

hist whist

hist   whist
little ghostthings
tip-toe
twinkle-toe

little twitchy
witches and tingling
goblins
hob-a-nob   hob-a-nob

little hoppy happy
toad in tweeds
tweeds
little itchy mousies

with scuttling
eyes   rustle and run   and
hidehidehide
whisk

whisk   look out for the old woman
with the wart on her nose
what she'll do to yer
nobody knows

for she knows the devil   ooch
the devil   ouch
the devil
ach   the great

green
dancing
devil
devil

devil
devil

      wheeEEE

e. e. cummings

Gobble-uns
and
Other Horrors

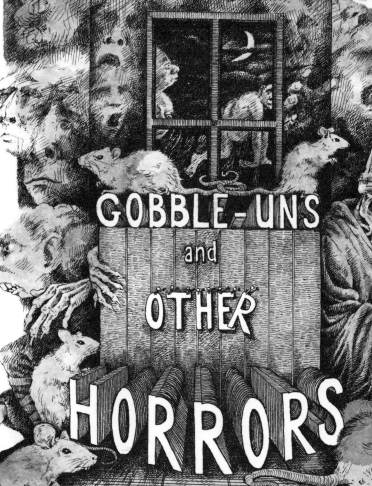

GOBBLE-UNS
and
OTHER
HORRORS

Little Orphant Annie

Little Orphant Annie's come to our house to stay,
An' wash the cups an' saucers up, an' brush the crumbs away,
An' shoo the chickens off the porch, an' dust the hearth,
      an' sweep,
An' make the fire, an' bake the bread, an' earn her
      board-an'-keep;
An' all us other childern, when the supper things is done,
We set around the kitchen fire an' has the mostest fun
A-list' nin' to the witch-tales 'at Annie tells about,
An' the Gobble-uns 'at gits you
    Ef you
        Don't
            Watch
                Out!

Onc't they was a little boy wouldn't say his prayers—
An' when he went to bed at night, away up stairs,
His mammy heerd him holler, an' his daddy heerd him bawl,
An' when they turn't the kivvers down, he wasn't there
      at all!
'An' they seeked him in the rafter-room, an' cubby-hole,
      an' press,
An' seeked him up the chimbly-flue, an' ever'wheres, I guess;
But all they ever found was thist his pants an' roundabout—
An' the Gobble-uns'll git you
    Ef you
        Don't
            Watch
                Out!

An' one time a little girl 'ud allus laugh an' grin,
An' make fun of ever' one, an' all her blood an' kin;
An' onc't, when they was 'company', an' ole folks was there,
She mocked 'em an' shocked 'em, an' said she didn't care!
An' thist as she kicked her heels, an' turn't to run an' hide,
They was two great big Black Things a-standin' by her side,
An' they snatched her through the ceilin' 'fore she
      knowed what she's about!
An' the Gobble-uns'll git you
    Ef you
        Don't
            Watch
                Out!

An' little Orphant Annie says, when the blaze is blue,
An' the lampwick sputters, an' the wind goes *woo-oo*!
An' you hear the crickets quit, an' the moon is gray,
An' the lightnin'-bugs in dew is all squenched away,—
You better mind yer parents, an' yer teachers fond
        an' dear,
An' churish them 'at loves you, an' dry the orphant's
        tear,
An' he'p the pore an' needy ones 'at clusters all about,
Er the Gobble-uns'll git you
    Ef you
       Don't
          Watch
            Out!

James Whitcomb Riley

The Troll

A troll once lived in a high pasture,
(A troll, a troll wife and their children too)
And one day there came a bold farmer
To speak with the troll as farmers do.

'Let us', he said, 'a bargain complete'
(A troll, a troll wife and their children too)
'I'll till this land, and what grows beneath
(This year I suggest a crop of wheat)
Shall be yours, Sir Troll, for this barren heath
Bears nothing that you can burn or eat.'
The troll, his troll wife and their children too
Were well enough pleased for the roots gave heat.

But the troll said 'Next year what's above the ground
Shall be mine'; so the farmer turnips planted
And the trolls an excellent salad made
Of the turnip leaves. But the farmer haunted

By his new found wealth and his old found greed,
(A troll, a troll wife and their children too)
A village with barns and a small church made
Where the church bells rang by night and day

And the troll, cursed out by the horrible sound,
With his family sadly trailed away.

Come summer and the farmer a feast prepared,
Rich, for his sole daughter was to be wed
But far on the heath an idiot boy
Met with the troll and the troll king said,

'This parcel, my son, be pleased to carry'
(A troll, a troll wife and their children too)
'It's a present for Farmer Will and his heir.'
It was icy cold and as lead heavy,
But the boy took it to the wedding pair.

And the parcel contained a lake, a lake
(A troll, a troll wife and their children too)
And it drowned all the company drinking there
Except for the boy who could swim like a swan
For a bargain was at stake, at stake
With a troll, a troll wife and their children.

Thomas Blackburn

145

Bishop Hatto

The summer and autumn had been so wet
That in winter the corn was growing yet;
'Twas a piteous sight to see all around
The grain lie rotting on the ground.

Every day the starving poor
Crowded around Bishop Hatto's door,
For he had a plentiful last-year's store,
And all the neighbourhood could tell
His granaries were furnish'd well.

At last Bishop Hatto appointed a day
To quiet the poor without delay;
He bade them to his great barn repair,
And they should have food for the winter there.

Rejoiced such tidings good to hear,
The poor folk flock'd from far and near;
The great barn was full as it could hold
Of women and children, and young and old.

Then when he saw it could hold no more,
Bishop Hatto he made fast the door,
And while for mercy on Christ they call,
He set fire to the barn and burnt them all.

'I' faith, 'tis an excellent bonfire!' quoth he,
'And the country is greatly obliged to me,
For ridding it in these times forlorn
Of rats, that only consume the corn.'

So then to his palace returned he,
And he sat down to supper merrily,
And he slept that night like an innocent man.
But Bishop Hatto never slept again.

In the morning as he enter'd the hall,
Where his pictures hung against the wall,
A sweat like death all over him came;
For the rats had eaten it out of the frame.

As he look'd there came a man from his farm,
He had a countenance white with alarm;
'My lord, I open'd your granaries this morn,
And the rats had eaten all your corn.'

Another came running presently,
And he was pale as pale could be;
'Fly! my Lord Bishop, fly!' quoth he,
'Ten thousand rats are coming this way—
The Lord forgive you for yesterday!'

Bishop Hatto fearfully hasten'd away,
And he crossed the Rhine without delay,
And reach'd his tower, and barr'd with care
All the windows, doors, and loopholes there.

He laid him down and closed his eyes,
But soon a scream made him arise;
He started, and saw two eyes of flame
On his pillows from whence the screaming came.

He listen'd and look'd; it was only the cat;
But the Bishop grew more fearful for that,
For she sat screaming, mad with fear,
At the army of rats that was drawing near.

For they have swum over the river so deep,
And they have climb'd the shores so steep,
And up the tower their way is bent,
To do the work for which they were sent.

They are not to be told by the dozen or score;
By thousands they come, and by myriads and more;
Such numbers had never been heard of before,
Such a judgement had never been witness'd of yore.

Down on his knees the Bishop fell,
And faster and faster his beads did he tell,
As louder and louder drawing near
The gnawing of their teeth he could hear.

And in at the windows, and in at the door,
And through the walls helter-skelter they pour,
And down from the ceiling, and up through the floor,
From the right and the left, from behind and before,
From within and without, from above and below,
And all at once to the Bishop they go.

They have whetted their teeth against the stones,
And now they pick the Bishop's bones;
They gnaw'd the flesh from every limb,
For they were sent to do judgement on him!

Robert Southey

The Hairy Toe

Once there was a woman went out to pick beans,
and she found a Hairy Toe.
She took the Hairy Toe home with her,
and that night, when she went to bed,
the wind began to moan and groan.
Away off in the distance
she seemed to hear a voice crying,
'Who's got my Hair-r-ry To-o-oe?
Who's got my Hair-r-ry To-o-oe?'

The woman scrooched down,
'way down under the covers,
and about that time
the wind appeared to hit the house,
smoosh,
and the old house creaked and cracked
like something was trying to get in.
The voice had come nearer,
almost at the door now,
and it said,
'Where's my Hair-r-ry To-o-oe?
Who's got my Hair-r-ry To-o-oe?'

The woman scrooched further down
under the covers
and pulled them tight around her head.
The wind growled around the house
like some big animal
and r-r-um-mbled
over the chimbley.
All at once she heard the door cr-r-a-ack
and Something slipped in
and began to creep over the floor.
The floor went
cre-e-eak, cre-e-eak
at every step that thing took towards her bed.
The woman could almost feel
it bending over her bed.
Then in an awful voice it said:
'Where's my Hair-r-ry To-o-oe?
Who's got my Hair-r-ry To-o-oe?
You've got it!'

Traditional American

The Bogeyman

In the desolate depths of a perilous place
the bogeyman lurks, with a snarl on his face.
Never dare, never dare to approach his dark lair
for he's waiting ... just waiting ... to get you.

He skulks in the shadows, relentless and wild
in his search for a tender, delectable child.
With his steely sharp claws and his slavering jaws
oh he's waiting ... just waiting ... to get you.

Many have entered his dreary domain
but not even one has been heard from again.
They no doubt made a feast for the butchering beast
and he's waiting ... just waiting ... to get you.

In that sulphurous, sunless and sinister place
he'll crumple your bones in his bogey embrace.
Never never go near if you hold your life dear,
for oh! ... what he'll do ... when he gets you!

Jack Prelutsky

The Mewlips

The shadows where the Mewlips dwell
    Are dark and wet as ink,
And slow and softly rings their bell,
    As in the slime you sink.

You sink into the slime, who dare
    To knock upon their door,
While down the grinning gargoyles stare
    And noisome waters pour.

Beside the rotting river-strand
    The drooping willows sweep,
And gloomily the gorcrows stand
    Croaking in their sleep.

Over the Merlock Mountains a long and weary way,
    In a mouldy valley where the trees are grey,
By a dark pool's borders without wind or tide,
    Moonless and sunless, the Mewlips hide.

The cellars where the Mewlips sit
    Are deep and dank and cold
With single sickly candle lit;
    And there they count their gold.

Their walls are wet, their ceilings drip;
    Their feet upon the floor
Go softly with a squish-flap-flip,
    As they sidle to the door.

They peep out slyly; through a crack
    Their feeling fingers creep,
And when they've finished, in a sack
    Your bones they take to keep.

Beyond the Merlock Mountains, a long and lonely road,
    Through the spider-shadows and the marsh of Tode,
And through the wood of hanging trees and the gallows-weed,
    You go to find the Mewlips—and the Mewlips feed.

J. R. R. Tolkien

The Trap

The first night that the monster lurched
Out of the forest on all fours,
He saw its shadow in his dream
Circle the house, as though it searched
For one it loved or hated. Claws
On gravel and a rabbit's scream
Ripped the fabric of his dream.

Waking between dark and dawn
And sodden sheets, his reason quelled
The shadow and the nightmare sound.
The second night it crossed the lawn
A brute voice in the darkness yelled.
He struggled up, woke raving, found
His wall-flowers trampled to the ground.

When rook wings beckoned the shadows back
He took his rifle down, and stood
All night against the leaded glass.
The moon ticked round. He saw the black
Elm-skeletons in the doomsday wood,
The sailing and the falling stars
And red coals dropping between bars.

The third night such a putrid breath
Fouled, flared his nostrils, that he turned,
Turned, but could not lift, his head.
A coverlet as thick as death
Oppressed him : he crawled out : discerned
Across the door his watchdog, dead.
'Build a trap', the neighbours said.

All that day he built his trap
With metal jaws and a spring as thick
As the neck of a man. One touch
Triggered the hanging teeth : jump, snap,
And lightning guillotined the stick
Thrust in its throat. With gun and torch
He set his engine in the porch.

The fourth night in their beds appalled
His neighbours heard the hunting roar
Mount, mount to an exultant shriek.
At daybreak timidly they called
His name, climbed through the splintered door,
And found him sprawling in the wreck,
Naked, with a severed neck.

Jon Stallworthy

Prayer

Grant that no Hobgoblins fright me,
No hungry devils rise up and bite me;
No Urchins, Elves or drunkard Ghosts
Shove me against walls or posts.

John Day

Index of Authors

Index of First Lines

Illustrators

Front Cover   Allan Curless
Visitors   Ian Miller
Transformations   Martin Lealan
Ghosts   David Parkins
Royal Persons   John Millington
Fairies and other Sprites   Biz Hull
Creatures   Daniel Woods
The Sea   Friere Wright
Music   Gwen Tourret
The Moon and Stars   Martin White
The Spirit of the Place   Friere Wright
Journeys and Struggles   Ian Miller
Magicians and Devils   John Millington
Gobble-uns and Other Horrors   Allan Curless

Acknowledgements

Dannie Abse: First published in *Tenants of the House* (Hutchinson). Reprinted by permission of Anthony Sheil Associates Ltd.

George Barker: From *To Aylsham Fair*. Reprinted by permission of Faber & Faber Ltd.

Thomas Blackburn: From *The Devil's Kitchen*. Reprinted by permission of Chatto & Windus Ltd.

Morris Bishop: From *Spilt Milk*. Copyright 1942, renewed © 1969 by Morris Bishop. Reprinted by permission of G. P. Putnam's Sons.

Charles Causley: 'Colonel Fazackerley' from *Figgie Hobbin*; 'Green Man in the Garden' and 'John Polruddon' from *Collected Poems* (both collections published by Macmillan). Reprinted by permission of David Higham Associates Ltd.

e.e. cummings: From *Complete Poems* (Granada) and also in *Tulips and Chimneys* (Liveright). Copyright 1923, 1925 and renewed 1951, 1953 by e.e. cummings. Copyright © 1973, 1976 by Nancy T. Andrews. Copyright © 1973, 1976 by George James Firmage. Reprinted by permission of Granada Publ. Ltd., and Liveright Publishing Corp.

Walter de la Mare: From *Collected Poems*. Reprinted by permission of The Literary Trustees of Walter de la Mare and The Society of Authors as their representative.

Emily Dickinson: Reprinted by permission of the publishers and the Trustees of Amherst College from *The Poems of Emily Dickinson*, edited by Thomas H. Johnson, Cambridge, Mass.: The Belknap Press of Harvard University Press, Copyright 1951, © 1955, 1979 by the President and Fellows of Harvard College.

W. Dunlop: From *Gallery* (edited by Margaret Greaves, Methuen Children's Books). Reprinted by permission of Associated Book Publishers Ltd.

Paul Edwards: From *A Ballad Book for Africa* (Faber). Reprinted by permission of the author.

Robert Frost: From *The Poetry of Robert Frost* (ed. by Edward Connery Lathem). Reprinted by permission of Jonathan Cape Ltd., for the editor and the Estate of Robert Frost, and by permission of Holt, Rinehart & Winston Inc.

Roland Gant: From *The Burning Thorn* (selected by Griselda Greaves, p.41). Reprinted by permission of Hamish Hamilton Ltd.

Phyllis Gotlieb: 'How and When and Where and Why' from "Ordinary Moving". Reprinted by permission of the author from *Ordinary Moving* (OUP Canada).

Robert Graves: 'Dicky' and 'The Alice Jean' from *The Penny Fiddle* (Cassell); 'The Two Witches' from *Collected Poems* (Cassell); 'Star Talk' first published in *Over The Brazier* (London, Poetry Bookshop 1916). All reprinted by permission of A. P. Watt Ltd.

Gregory Harrison: Reprinted by permission from *The Night of the Wild Horses* (Oxford University Press). © Gregory Harrison 1971.

Miroslav Holub: From *Miroslav Holub: Selected Poems*, trans. Ian Milner and George Theiner (Penguin Modern European Poets, 1967, p.45). Copyright © Miroslav Holub, 1967. Translation copyright © Penguin Books, 1967. Reprinted by permission of Penguin Books Ltd.

Ted Hughes: 'Foxgloves' from *The Earth Owl*, and 'Moon Whales' from *Moon Bells and Other Poems*, published by Chatto & Windus. Reprinted by permission of Faber & Faber Ltd.

James Joyce: The poem entitled 'Chamber Music' is No. V, "Lean out of the Window ..." from *Chamber Music*. Reprinted by permission of Jonathan Cape Ltd., for the Executors of the James Joyce Estate.

Rudyard Kipling: From *Rewards and Fairies*. Reprinted by permission of A. P. Watt Ltd. for the National Trust and Macmillan London Ltd.

James Kirkup: First published in *Round About Nine* (ed. Geoffrey Palmer and Noel Lloyd, Frederick Warne, 1976). Reprinted by permission of Dr. Jan Van Loewen Ltd.

Laurence Lerner: From *The Directions of Memory*. Reprinted by permission of Chatto & Windus Ltd.

C. S. Lewis: From *Poems*. Reprinted by permission of Collins Publishers.

Vachel Lindsay: From *Collected Poems*. Copyright 1920 by Macmillan Publishers Co. Inc., renewed 1948 by Elizabeth C. Lindsay. Reprinted by permission of Macmillan Publ. Co. Inc.

John Masefield: From *Poems* (Macmillan). Copyright 1930 and renewed 1958 by John Masefield. Reprinted by permission of The Society of Authors as the literary representative of the Estate of John Masefield, and Macmillan Publ. Co. Inc., New York.

Harold Monro: From *The Silent Pool* (Duckworth).

Ogden Nash: From *Many Long Years Ago*. Copyright 1936 by Ogden Nash. Reprinted by permission of A. P. Watt Ltd., for the Estate of Ogden Nash, and of Little, Brown & Co.

Brian Patten: From *Notes to the Hurrying Man*. Reprinted by permission of George Allen & Unwin (Publ.) Ltd.

Jack Prelutsky: From *Nightmares: Poems to Trouble Your Sleep*. Text copyright © by Jack Prelutsky. Reprinted by permission of A. & C. Black Ltd., and of Greenwillows Books (A Division of Wiliam Morrow & Co.).

James Reeves: 'The Old Wife and the Ghost', 'The Three Singing Birds' and 'Toadstool Wood' all from *The Blackbird in the Lilac* (1952). Reprinted by permission of Oxford University Press. 'The Bogus Boo' from *More Prefabulous Animiles* and 'Little Fan' from *The Wandering Moon*. Both reprinted by permission of William Heinemann Ltd.

Alastair Reid: From *Shadows and Spells* (ed. Barbara Ireson, Faber). Reprinted by permission of the author.

E. V. Rieu: 'The Paint Box' was first published in *A Puffin Quartet of Poets* (1958); 'The Unicorn' was first published in *Cuckoo Calling* (Methuen 1933).

T. G. Roberts: From *The Leather Bottle*. Reprinted by permission of McGraw-Hill Ryerson Ltd., Toronto.

Vita Sackville-West: Song from "*Mirage*" from *Collected Poems* (Hogarth Press). Reprinted by kind permission of Curtis Brown Ltd. on behalf of The Estate of Victoria Sackville-West.

Geoffrey Scott: First published in *A Box of Paints* (London 1923). By permission of Marchesa Iris Origo, Geoffrey Scott's Literary Executor.

Ian Serraillier: From *Happily Ever After* (Oxford University Press). Copyright © 1963 Ian Serraillier. Reprinted by permission of the author.

Edith Sitwell: From *Collected Poems* (Macmillan). Reprinted by permission of David Higham Associates Ltd.

Osbert Sitwell: 'Evening' from *Poems about People*; 'Tom' from *Selected Poems: Old and New* (Duckworth). Reprinted by permission of David Higham Associates Ltd.

C. L. Smith: From *The Old Merlaine*. Reprinted by permission of William Heinemann Ltd.

Stevie Smith: From *Collected Poems* (Allen Lane). Reprinted by kind permission of James MacGibbon as Literary Executor.

Jon Stallworthy: From *The Apple Barrel* © Oxford University Press 1961, 1963). Reprinted by permission of Oxford Univ. Press.

James Stephens: From *Collected Poems*. Reprinted by permission of Mrs. Iris Wise and Macmillan, London and Basingstoke.

Efua Sutherland: From *Messages: Poems from Ghana* (ed. by Awoonor and Adali-Mortty). Reprinted by permission of Heinemann Educational Books Ltd.

J. R. R. Tolkien: 'Far Over the Misty Mountains'; 'Under the Mountain Dark and Tall'; and 'The Wind Was on the Withered Heath', all from *The Hobbit*. 'Mewlips' from *The Adventurer of Tom Bombadil* All reprinted by permission of George Allen & Unwin (Publ.) Ltd.

W. J. Turner: From *The Hunter and other poems*. Reprinted by permission of Sidgwick & Jackson Ltd.

R. Wilson: From *Rhyme and Rhythm-Yellow Book* (ed. Gibson & Wilson). Reprinted by permission of Macmillan, London and Basingstoke.

Judith Wright: From *Selected Poems—Five Senses*. © Judith Wright 1963. Reprinted by pemission of Angus & Robertson (UK) Ltd.

W. B. Yeats: From *Collected Poems*. Reprinted by permission of A. P. Watt Ltd., for M.B. Yeats, Anne Yeats and the publishers, Macmillan London Ltd.